Praise for You Belong Here

I was all the way sucked in by the introduction. Overcoming addiction, depression, moving from her South African home to Korea and coming out as her authentic lgbtq+ self in spite of Christian upbringing. Khanyisa Mnyaka is a true expert in authenticity, her story is told with humor and grace.

— Tess Cruz Foley, author of *Mindfully Inclusive*, founder of Brave Space Consulting

Discovering self-love is essential to true happiness. Khanyisa's courageous journey to self-acceptance will be a light to anyone who feels they don't belong.

— Mimi Rich, MA Marriage and Family Therapist

You Belong Here: Your Roadmap to Confidence, Purpose, and Authenticity by Khanyisa Mnyaka is a powerful and transformative book that every woman should read. Khanyisa's personal journey from a place of deep despair, confusion, and self-doubt to a position of strength, purpose, and self-acceptance is nothing short of inspiring. Her story of breaking free from societal expectations, religious dogma, and the fear of judgment is a testament to the resilience of the human spirit.

This book is a guide to self-discovery, self-love, and reclaiming your true self. It challenges you to dig deep into your past, confront your inner demons, and find the courage to live authentically.

Khanyisa's emphasis on the importance of self-trust, self-awareness, and self-acceptance resonates on a profound level. The thought-provoking questions at the end of each chapter provide a valuable opportunity for introspection and growth.

You Belong Here is not just a book; it's a roadmap for any woman seeking to break free from the chains of societal expectations and discover her true purpose. It's a call to embrace radical self-love and live unapologetically. Khanyisa's message is one of empowerment, and her book is a powerful tool for any woman looking to embark on a transformational journey towards a more confident, purposeful, and authentic life. Read it and begin your own path to self-discovery and fulfillment.

— SHAWNA BURKHOLDER, AUTHOR OF *FIERCE AWAKENINGS*

I must commend the author on her exceptional writing style. The prose is not only elegant but also immersive, creating a vivid tapestry of imagery and emotion throughout the narrative. The ability of the author to craft sentences and articulate ideas is truly commendable, making the reading experience thoroughly enjoyable. The combination of English and native South African language in narration is engaging.

The character development in the book is outstanding. Each character felt authentic and well-rounded, with motivations and flaws that added depth to the overall story. I found myself deeply invested in their journeys, and the way you brought them to life made the narrative incredibly engaging.

This book is a must read book for all, the book will serve as an inspiration, especially to those who can't make decisions because they are afraid and ashamed of what people will think about their actions. The author discussed relevant themes affecting our society. Themes like societal prejudice and sentiments, sexual abuse, gender discrimination and the way of life of certain people in Africa.

Moreover, the pacing of the plot was masterful. The way the author structured the story kept me eagerly turning the pages, and the seamless integration of twists and turns added an exciting layer of unpredictability. It's evident that the author put a considerable amount of thought into the plot, and the result is a narrative that is both gripping and thought-provoking.

— PATRICIA KYLE, EDITOR

You Belong Here

Your Roadmap to Confidence, Purpose and Authenticity

Khanyisa Mnyaka

YOU
BELONG
HERE

YOUR ROADMAP TO CONFIDENCE, PURPOSE, AND AUTHENTICITY

KHANYISA MNYAKA

Red Thread Publishing LLC. 2024

Write to info@redthreadbooks.com if you are interested in publishing with Red Thread Publishing. Learn more about publications or foreign rights acquisitions of our catalog of books: www.redthreadbooks.com

Paperback ISBN: 978-1-955683-99-9

Ebook ISBN: 978-1-955683-95-1

Cover Design: Red Thread Designs

For my mother and the life she did not get to LIVE

CONTENTS

FOREWORD

When Khanyisa and I first met at the United Nations University for Peace in 2013, we deeply bonded over our love for music, cheap boxed wine, and social justice. We found each other again a decade later, bonding now in our practices of spirituality, self-love... and still a deep love of social justice.

When she asked me to write this forward I was floored. How could I even begin to share what this human has meant to me, what this book has meant to me, and what she has meant to so many people through her love, her stories, her work, and mostly through her ways of being?

I shall do my best. I will fail.

And that is the dance of life.

What Khanyisa has just handed you here is a gift. I implore you, do not let this pass you by. *This is NOT another self-help book.* This is a deep archeological dig into the spirituality of self-discovery from a woman raised in a village turned small town in South Africa, rooting in her first language of isiXhosa, traveling the world to meet a truer, more connected version of herself again and again and again. A modern-day personal version of *The Alchemist*, Khanyisa has dedicated this book to her mother and the life she did not get to live. Her words also speak to the mother in us all that has shut down our life's dreams due to the perceived or actual need to pay the bills, just get by for this day or this week or this month... only to get back in the cycle once again.

As an American-born, educated, white presenting, "spiritual" woman I have OFTEN found myself in the rat race that has me buckle down my experience, ignore any uncomfortable feelings, and put my needs and wants on the wayside in order to just make it through today. To do what needs to be done to write that paper. Pay the bills. Show up for someone or something else. Feed the children. Show up for my family.

I have often been the one I leave behind. Then, as the great pendulum swing of life goes, I have often overemphasized my own pain, my own self-abandonment in spaces where collective trauma is being expressed, in places where other's oppression is begging to be centered. Here comes my personal lack of a village, mentors, and a connection with the earth has had me, again and again, center myself. Especially in capitalist, western-oriented "spiritual" work.

This book CUTS into the heart of this cycle of self-neglect, and critiques the capitalistic-based spiritual work that leads to over self-centering. Khanyisa does this through a raw process of RADICAL self-honesty and a return to listening to the Earth's wisdom as an act of self-love, while also including spiritual contemplation of how we can organize and create solidarity with the most oppressed in our world. This book is a vulnerable documentation of some of the most intimate fuck-ups and traumas a human can go through. From personal battles with addiction, physical abuse, and sexual abuse, to becoming a dominating role in others' lives, Khanyisa breaks down what it truly means to love ourselves THROUGH it by being honest about what we have done, how we felt and feel, and what we are committed to being a stand for especially in the shit we go through and the shit we have been the cause of.

This book dives deep into the question of following our heart or surviving in a capitalist world that if you don't pay attention, you could end up on the streets. As Khanyisa shows again and again, this truth is now global, from South Africa to South Korea, from Costa Rica to the United States of America. The wrong paperwork, not enough money to pay the bills, the wrong passport stamp, and the wrong comment, could lead anyone of us, without a home, job, friends, family, or even national identity. The tender fabric of the transactional reality that we humans have created is so pointedly explored through personal, familiar, and collective story and highlights the great GAP that we currently find ourselves straddling. What is more important? Life? Or working to play catch up to a capitalist image of success?

Our generational trauma gets played out in our interpersonal relationships and that is where we get hurt and hurt others the most. Khanyisa does NOT shy away from honesty in her journey of being the one who has witnessed and received so much pain and also caused pain in the name of untouched personal and generational trauma. She also dives deep into her Xhosa culture and the identity of a Black South African, the modern collective fear of being labeled a witch, having to deeply compensate to prove oneself as a "woman of faith" and the extraordinary pressure of to conform that is placed on the global majority (women and children of color) to appear "more normal" than any other identity.

Khanyisa painfully and poetically dives into the fear that drives so many of us around self-discovery, expression, and standing up for what is truly right - "What will people say?" How much have you said no when you meant yes, and yes when you meant no, in the name of the "public's" (your family, your parents, your social media following, etc) opinions? How much have you abandoned yourself in the name of others' potential stories about you? The recovering people pleaser in me had to breathe deeply with this one. Because the truth is, after a few hours, maybe weeks at the most, people actually don't give a shit.

And the reality check in the middle of our self-discovery is that our personal suffering is also connected to our collective suffering due to the over-extraction of natural resources, patriarchy, white supremacy, capitalism, racism, ableism, heteronormativity and more weave a through line in Khanyisa's words. The loss of her own, once safe & communal village as it grew into a small town where everyone had to be home by dusk or live (or die) in the consequences of brutal night activity sets the stage for her deep dive into the human psyche of identity, love, trauma, healing and a remembering of our wholeness. The deep dive into how colonial Christianity influenced and depleted the traditional Xhosa culture as the transition of her grandfather's life also marked the end of thousands-year-old rituals. Enter high school and the deep self-shaming that followed with her identity as a lesbian AND a Christian, two truths that lived as a painful paradox most of her young adult life. And, in the midst of all of this, what I find MOST fascinating and admirable is Khanyisa's ability to take personal responsibility for her actions while also naming the systems of oppression that have created the patterns of domination and oppression in her and in all of our lives.

Sex. Sexuality. Aids. In South Africa in the 1990s, at the height of the African aids 'epidemic' and at the tail end of the apartheid regime, Khanysya paints us a personal and cultural narrative of the shame of sex and the discomfort of the entire cultural stature to try to explain safety in sex to children in a world deeply imbued with domestic sexual violence and the normalization of incest. Yes, it isn't "Africa" it has become the WORLD that is deep in the trauma of sex and sexuality. Khanyisa's personal story is not exclusive to the children of South Africa. I also deeply relate to her story of familial sexual abuse and, at the time this was written, more than 60% of American women admit to being unwillingly sexualized by a family member before the age of 18. Once again, her honest personal narrative highlights a collective trauma.

Khanyisa also gives deep spiritual insight into her relationship with the love, the force, God, Goddess, the one life that lives us all while also deconstructing the colonial experience of Christianity in her personal life. Even as you read some of the horrific experiences this human has witnessed and gone through, her steady return to the one energy of goodness, God, love, whatever it is called, makes her a hero. This hope, this knowing that there is a life that is living us and is greater than us, and loves us deeply, and we can connect to it when we get still & quiet enough continues to give me hope for this moment and for the future.

In the dire time where genocide is normalized and were told that enslavement of children is needed in order for us to have our cell phones and if we want to warm our houses then we'll have to put up with the sea rising... there is hope.

This self-love that Khanyisa speaks of is not a 'yoga mat and crystal' la-la land of fantasy. It is the fierce grace of getting radically honest with ourselves, loving this life deeply, and being willing to take a stand in the face of those who are deep in their own destructive patterns of dominating others due to their untouched trauma.

This book is a practice in empathy building. This book is a guide deep into the soul of what it means to be human.

This book is a map of PRACTICES for the lost, tired, traumatized child, in order to find your way to a self-loving, caring, imperfect, wise adult.

I invite you to think of this more like that, a map, a workbook, a place for you to traverse the beauty and the pain of your own life and come out in deeper rapport with yourself and the trauma that we as humans all share.

Before we can meet in love, we must be honest about our shared grief.

I hope you enjoy this map back to self-love, self-compassion, and a collectively shared journey into the soul that now Life-Coach Khanyisa conveys here so intimately, poetically, and RAW. A deeply personal journey of the collective human story. The continual choice to return to your own soul.

Con amor y solidaridad,
   Reverend Briana Lynn

INTRODUCTION

Have you ever gone through a depression so dark that it feels like there is no way out? A darkness so incredibly hollow, that the only way you can escape it is by pretending like it doesn't exist. The type of heavy sadness that has no explanation, no reason, and when you try to tell people about it, you don't even know where to start because what do you say? No fatalities, no injuries, yet this oppressive depression has made its home in your heart, leaving you no choice but to contemplate escaping it through death. But, you know you don't really want to die, there is something about living that you enjoy but you know that something has to die for you to fully participate in life again. I'm talking about the type of depression that makes you dread going to bed with the same amount of intensity you dread waking up. This is the depression where you feel like something you've done, at some point in time has finally caught up with you and this darkness and depression are its revenge. You know what I'm talking about, it feels like you owe life a debt and this depression is the Italian gangster it has sent to collect. You have also learned how to live your life with this darkness, you function, you half-heartedly participate and what people think is a cute crooked smile is literally a half smile. Come on, you know what I'm talking about, the depression that fucks with your relationship with food whether you eat to fill the void or you have lost any sense of your hunger cues. Where your reflection in the mirror feels contorted, it looks like you are looking at yourself through still water but no, it is the mirror in the bathroom only what you see, you do not recognize.

It is this type of darkness and depression that had me looking for an English teaching job in South Korea. The masking, the chameleon behavior, the numbing, all of it wasn't working anymore. I was a closeted homosexual, living as a born-again Christian, unemployable, broke, and oh so alone. In the midst of the overwhelming darkness, and depression, a glimmer of hope emerged. Not just out of the depression and pain, but out of the pretending, out of the forced heterosexuality, out of the unaligned friendships, out of the toxic family relationship, out of all of it. The suitcase carried the clothes I no longer wanted to wear, while the backpack held a journal I was going to use to write about this glorious escape and my heart, while my heart carried hope and fear with unexplainable efficiency. I landed in South Korea cloaked in a heavy trench coat because it was June, and winter in South Africa, but it was the peak of summer in South Korea. The heaviness of that coat felt like a physical manifestation of what was going on in my heart and soul. Heavy. What I thought would be an escape from the depression proved me so wrong. Imagine my confusion when I cried myself to sleep that first night in South Korea. A familiar feeling washed over me like an avalanche. There it was, here, with me, in this new country, on this new bed, with these new people... the depression. Fuck. I hadn't escaped it, I hadn't fixed it. In fact, now I had added the complication of a foreign country where I was the only Black person in my rural town, Joengkok. What was the depression trying to show me? I mean I knew, I was just scared to look, it was showing me....EVERYTHING.

I spent every single weekend of my first six months in South Korea drunk. Alcohol became a numbing mechanism that I gladly embraced, serving as a bandage I'd use to cover the festering wounds of shame, hurt, confusion and loss. I have weekends that I cannot remember, memories just wiped out by the amount of alcohol I had consumed.

Sometimes, I get flashbacks, like that one time I threw up in a cab and the driver made my friend clean it up or that time I leaned over the escalator in Seoul and threw up on the people below. I also remember those dreaded morning apologies I would have to make when I would piece together the night, recalling all the inappropriate things I said and did. Alcohol was such a big part of my South Korea stories, and even beyond. I've been sober for almost a year now and I have to tell you, alcohol isn't the best vice for depression, it is actually the worst. When the temporary weekend numbing faded and I had to face myself on Monday morning, it would feel like the depression had multiplied. My Mondays felt like a breeding ground for self-loathing, regret, and a deep sense of worthlessness. I regretted everything: the amount of alcohol I drank, the things I said and did, the hangover that would last a full two days, and who I was becoming. Growing up in a household where most of the men were alcoholics, I had promised myself that that would never be my story. The thought that I was becoming like them haunted me but alcohol was the only thing that made things feel kind of okay.

I sat with a friend on one of these alcohol-led evenings in Itaewon, our preferred party district in Seoul. Unprovoked and prophetic, my friend said "You know, you get to be who you are here. You are new now, you can even change your name if you want to." At first, I wanted to defend myself, but what about me that made him think I wasn't being myself and needed to change my name!? Before I said anything, I glanced at the short little skirt I kept pulling down each time I got up, the dangling earrings I uncomfortably decorated my ears with, and the top that showed my beautiful cleavage in ways I would have preferred it not to. Maybe my friend saw the discomfort, or maybe I got too excited when I told him about that one time I had a secret girlfriend in the church. I don't know what he saw or heard, but he told me something I needed to hear. I could be whoever I want to be! But what I realized more than that is that...I could be ME! You see, up until that point, I was just everything everyone said I should be. When I was a young girl, I was a version of myself that would appease my grandmother; as a teenager, I was whoever the church found acceptable, as a young adult, I worked to be all things to all people. I had done such an amazing job disappearing into who I needed to be at a given moment that I had convinced myself that all these collected versions were the real me. This conversation with my friend was the permission slip I craved to loosen the grip of expectation, break free from the box of conformity, and become who I am.

I don't remember the first time I said "I'm gay, or a lesbian," I can't see a specific person who I looked in the eye and say, "I am gay." I just remember being. This is what my friend meant: I could just live, be, self-define, self-actualize. This was the type of liberation he was telling me I had and without even knowing, gave me permission to live in. I had been in a same-sex relationship before this but forced myself back into the closet when we got caught (more on this later). South Korea was the first time I owned my identity, allowed myself the privilege of living as me. It was the first time I had a deep comprehension of what Oprah and all the other self-development thought leaders were talking about when they would urge us to live as the truest versions of ourselves. The biggest barrier in that journey is our lack of bravery, our lack of awareness of the stories that have shackled us and made us prisoners of a culture that benefits from our conformity and fears we are afraid to face because we know what we stand to lose should we dare to be us. My journey of empowerment didn't begin and end with me struggling with my sexuality. Owning my sexual identity played a significant role in my journey towards liberation but it was one of the many hills I had to climb to fully embrace a vibrant and fulfilling existence. I had spent so much of my life existing, surviving, sharing stories of victimhood and self-pity that coming out was just the tip of the iceberg.

There is so much that adds to this human experience: our religious beliefs, our cultural norms, our schooling, our trauma, and those deep-rooted belief systems. All of these serve as burial grounds for our true authenticity and in order for us to truly LIVE, we have to roll up our sleeves and start digging. This book is your first shovel in that digging process. "You Belong Here, LIVE" is a gentle war cry to help you get back to the land of the living. It is a call for you to participate, to engage, to take up space in your life. It is a reminder that you are the MVP here, and you've been on the sidelines for way too long. This is your roadmap back to you, back to the parts of you that this society and the shitty shit that life has thrown at you stole. Your power, your confidence, and your authenticity. This is my only ask: as you read, please engage. Have your highlighter and pen ready, do the journaling parts of the book. When you read, be in a quiet place so that you can be present with you. Yes, this book uses my life and experience as anecdotes but the most important thing is that you are not afraid to reflect.

ONE

LIVE, PASSIONATELY

"Follow your passion, be prepared to work hard and sacrifice, and, above all, don't let anyone limit your dreams."

— DONOVAN BAILEY, FAMOUS OLYMPIC ATHLETE
AND AUTHOR OF UNDISPUTED: A CHAMPION'S LIFE

My Uncle Anele, the youngest of my mother's nine siblings, was undoubtedly the best sports man in our town during his high school career. With only an eight-year age gap between the two of us, I remember Anele's high school career very well. I also know that he was the best sportsman in our town because Cala is very small. Cala was one of those villages that somehow morphed into small towns over time. Ours is one of the first families in town and I know about the evolution of the town through my grandmother's lamentation about how things have changed but not for the better. I have been privy to the change as well, and it has not been pleasant. What once was a safe village turned small town is now an unsafe place where one has to be at home with the gates locked before dusk.

Due to the size of our town, we all know each other, about each other and sometimes, we know too much about each other. There is no hiding in Cala, no secret that will not be exposed. It was from the streets of my village-like town where I found out that one of my three sisters was in fact my mother - a secret my grandmother fought tooth and nail to keep from me. I was walking into a store when someone proclaimed "Yho, uyakhula lomntana kaVuyeka" (Wow, Vuyeka's child is growing up). The secret my grandparents labored for years to keep was now told to me by a passing stranger who happened to know things about my family. Well, the truth is that I already knew this. My grandparents were way too old to have a child my age, especially my grandfather. I was around nine years old when the stranger told me "the truth" but I knew she had revealed something I was not supposed to know, so I continued to feign my ignorance.

We know these types of secrets about each other's families. Sometimes, when my grandmother and I were sitting outside on the veranda, she would tell me random things about the people passing by. "Uyambona lo Khanyisa, uyinto efana wena" (You see that one Khanyisa, she is just like you). It was confusing at first, being told that people I didn't really know were "just like me." But now I know, it means children born outside of marriage. Children whose fathers had to be convinced that they were indeed the father. Children whose mothers were too young to birth them. Children who had to be raised by their grandparents because their own (parents) were not old enough to be parents. There are a lot of us like this in Cala, and my grandmother knows a lot of them.

Cala is also so small that I tell people if they ever find themselves lost in Cala, for some reason, all they need to do is go to any store or gas station and tell them my last name. It won't take more than that to find us. If, for example, you asked someone at the Spar supermarket, they would tell you to cross the road and keep going straight, we are the third house before you get to the clinic. Apart from knowing each other's poorly kept secrets, we know each other's gifts and talents as well.

Lonwabo, the boy from across the road, whose parents were my aunt and uncle because the father had the same clan name as my grandmother, was known for his genius and his cowardice. You'd often see Lonwabo sprinting home from school, avoiding a bully who'd challenged him to an after-school fist fight for no reason whatsoever! It was therefore genius of him to associate with the bullies, thus securing his protection from ...the bullies. I was mad that I didn't think of that myself. My bullies tormented me throughout primary and elementary school. My fresh cow milk and freshly baked bread were devoured before lunch break by the tallest boy in class. I was an easy target too - the youngest, shortest, and shyest person in the class. Lonwabo's plan was a display of sheer genius: I think he offered class notes in return for his protection. It is no surprise to any of us that Lonwabo is now a doctor - the only doctor that my grandmother would see in town.

The tallest girl in my school was disappointed at netball but pleasantly surprised at softball. The teachers at my primary school were not impressed with her choosing softball over netball. Each year, the netball coach would try to get her to play; there was nothing they could do with her inability to make the net. They assumed that because she was tall, she would be an excellent shooter but that simply was not the case. Her strong right arm made her an instant success when softball was introduced to the school. I tried both softball and netball in fact but was just okay in both. Not too bad that I couldn't play but also not good enough to make every game. Thembela was the star of the team; she would sometimes hit the ball so hard that it would go over the fence and the rest of us would stroll to home base. I think about how that wasn't impressive to the adults around us. They thought she should be good at netball and whatever else she did was just not enough. Teachers and parents play an active role in creating the voices in our heads that tell us that we are not good enough.

Some of the messages are subliminal. It's in the "you should and you shouldn't." "You should be smarter, faster, stronger and since you aren't, you are not good enough." My math teacher once hit me for not being smarter than everyone else in class. I didn't fail the test, I just didn't do as well as she expected me to do. She called out my name and handed me the test results; right as I was reaching out for it, she slapped me on both sides of my face with an open hand. A grown woman slapping a child across the face, how did this shit become okay? I was not even the smartest kid in the class, you know, the one who never gets less than 100 percent in every test. But here I was, my face turned red and my body shaking because this teacher felt like "I could have done better." I know she probably thought she was encouraging me, giving me tough love but she made me hate math. Forget the fact that I could have had a logical reason for not doing as well as I usually do but, instead of talking, she beat the shit out of me. If she'd asked, I would have told her how we ran out of candles while I was studying that night. Without knowing my situation, this teacher decided to inflict pain on my body, thus inflicting pain on my spirit and adding to my struggle with shame. I also never failed another math test after that, never. This teacher had put the fear of *her* in me. However, I also didn't enjoy math, which explains why I dropped it as soon as I was given the option in high school. I wasn't learning from a place of curiosity but rather fear. Fear of being singled out, fear of being shamed and fear of being punished.

Back to the talents of my small but busy town, Siya was known for her angelic voice. The room would fall into complete silence when she sang. She held a note in ways that were humanly impossible. All her performances were followed by oohs and ahhhs of appreciation; forget getting a solo when she was around. Everyone in her family could sing, but not in the "all Black people can sing" situation, but they could all SING! Her mother was the head music teacher in our primary school, both Siya and her brother were stars of the school choir. She would start each song with a vibrato that made birds sound like amateurs, the Italian words from the opera songs flowed out of her mouth as if she was born speaking the language and she knew what she was saying. Of course she didn't, we were only eleven years old and could barely speak English. We were not in the least bit surprised when we heard of her admission to the opera school and her booming career as an opera vocalist. Siya has performed in world-class stages, lived the life that she imagined because she was allowed to follow her passion.

Anele, my uncle, dominated the sports world (well, town in this case) all throughout his high school career. Anele was a jack of all trades and master of all when it came to sports! Name a sport, and he could play it. His name was chanted during the Olympic Games and even contact sports. My grandmother said he was just born physically strong. She would gloat about how she doesn't remember a time when he didn't have a six-pack. A natural athlete whose form screamed that he was set to be successful in any sports of his choosing. I clearly remember one morning, when a grocery delivery boy purposely ran him over with his delivery bicycle. Let me describe the bicycle for you so this all makes sense. It's one of those old-school, iron-made bicycles with an iron-made basket. These baskets were made to hold 12.5 kgs of maize meal, flour, corn and sacks of potatoes - all at the same time.

What I am saying is that this was a strong-ass bicycle. Anyway, it was a known fact that the delivery boy and Anele were not particularly friends. So, this morning, the boy mustered up some courage by trying to run Anele over with his bicycle. Instead, he was the one who fell over; the strength in Anele's legs sent him flying off the bike and asking for forgiveness because he knew he wouldn't win a fist fight. Anele walked tall, his shoulders broad and legs curved; imagine a swimmer's back and the legs of a soccer player if you will. He was even excellent at random shit, like high jump, javelin throwing, shotput and everything that had to do with physical strength. As if that wasn't enough, he was gifted with an amazing singing voice, a talent he willingly shared with both the school and church choirs. There was no "off-season" for my uncle; he participated in every extracurricular activity that he could.

However, rugby and boxing were his ultimate favorites. He was compared to the infamous Jonah Lomu of the New Zealand All Blacks when he played rugby. He played the same position as the legend and rugby enthusiasts in my town couldn't stop gushing over how similar their local talent played just like Jonah. I didn't even know who Jonah Lomu was until much later in life, but I knew that he must be something special because my uncle glowed every time his name was mentioned in the same sentence as Jonah. Sporting events were never really my cup of tea but my family made such a big deal about them that I would find myself watching rugby and pointing him to my friends "that's my uncle!" I saw him gallop around that rugby field with what I thought was a weirdly shaped ball at the time. I watched him run and push until he would enthusiastically throw him on the ground and the chants from the crowd would ensue when he got up.

The town made up a chant for him during all his boxing matches "val'umnyango angabaleki." His fans would sing, wide smiles as their champ jumped up and down the ring waiting for his match to begin.

The song means "close the door so that he doesn't run." It was made up during a match when an opponent ran out of the ring when he saw my uncle's boxing stance and physique. His love for sports ran so deep that he built his own punching bag in the kraal using cow dung and an empty potato sack. We would watch him shadow box while taking a bath; we used small round basins. He would wash the top half of his body in front of everyone and then move to a private room after (just thought I'd clear that up). I hope I've painted a clear picture for you of just how much my Uncle Anele loved boxing.

I was so sure he would be as famous as Mike Ncitha, his boxing idol from the same province as us. I vividly recall the day that Mike visited our town. I don't think my uncle slept a wink the night prior. Mike was there to scout for local talent and my uncle was one of the boys on his watch. My grandfather, too, remained awake late into the night, imparting his boxing wisdom to my uncle. They forged a special bond, fueled by their shared passion for the sport. We used to wake up early some Saturday mornings to watch the American greats like Mohammed Ali and Evander Holyfield. My grandfather, enthralled by the brilliance of his favorite boxer, would form his fists and uncontrollably move side-to-side in his chair as if he were the one fighting. My uncle would be next to him doing the same.

Anele had all that talent and passion for sport but he didn't have any academic excellence. He did "just okay" in all his academic subjects and almost failed in some. I wouldn't say he was the lowest scoring in class at all, but he was lower than average; making it through to the next grade by the skin of his teeth. After my grandfather died, my grandmother sent Anele to live with his older brother to get him away from these "crazy" sports and focus on his books. She called boxing "umdlalo wendlavini" (a rascal's sport). It worked. That was the year Anele stopped playing any sports. He would come back to our town for school breaks and there was no more shadow boxing and the cow dung punching bag was no longer hanging in the kraal. One thing didn't change though, Anele was still not an academic genius. His school report didn't suddenly have all A+.

What my grandmother knew about success was that only people with an education were entitled to it. By some luck and partial effort,

Anele managed to get good enough grades to get into a technical college. My grandmother broke her back, working to make sure Anele went to study IT (Information Technology), in Pretoria. Pretoria, a ten-hour bus ride from Cala! She was a prison cook making six hundred rands a month (sixty American dollars). She borrowed money from loan sharks, friends and even started a pig-selling side hustle. Anele went from being a village boy, shadow boxing in the living room, to living in the city to study I.T. He couldn't even use a computer - schools in the villages don't have computers and he was expected to kick ass at Information Technology! Forsaking all he knew, all his talents and passions, Anele made that long trip to Pretoria because, after three years, he would get a diploma in I.T. and he would make a lot of money.

It is such a conundrum, isn't it? The choice between passion and money/safety. We live in a world that has made us believe that the latter is worth sacrificing the former. We are socialized to believe that passion doesn't lead to survival. In doing research for this chapter; I found that a lot of people googled this very question; should I choose my passion over what I know will make money? This is a difficult question. It is also a difficult choice to make and that is why 84% of working adults are doing jobs they absolutely abhor. It is also why your family lost their shit when you told them you wanted to be an artist and now you are working at some government office and daydreaming about spending your days covered in paint. Or you waking up on a Monday morning with that overwhelming dread because being a lawyer just isn't you. Or you spend precious hours of your life studying medicine because your dad said "this is what we do in this family, we are doctors" but you would rather travel around India learning Hindi and googling "how to cure food poisoning." Majority of us have submitted to these lives, submitted to a point where we have forgotten about those passions and chugged them off as "childish desires." While a few have gone ahead and explored the question, then proceeded to forcefully pursue their passions.

I also recognize that it is an absolute privilege to live a life that is in unwavering pursuit of your passions. It is not an easy thing to do for a lot of people, and for some, it is nearly impossible. Choice is not available to all of us and we have to reckon. Exploring questions that make one seem "selfish, ungrateful, and self-centered" is not an option for most people. When you allow yourself the grace to sit with these big questions, it might be that you are in a space that is loving or that you are alone. It also means that you are empowered or have empowered yourself to choose. You are at an advantage because you are experiencing what I call **self-identification** and **self-defining**. Self-identification is the process of saying "this is who I am," "this is what I want," "this is how I choose to lead my life." It is the moment of self-revelation that disempowers anything that tries to make you less authentic. This is that powerful gift of telling people who YOU are. When you are not able to self-identify, others will identify for you. You will be told who you are, what you should do, who you should marry, when you should marry, when you should have children, and the list is endless. You will be in a constant state of being an infant, waiting to be given direction by those you appointed (knowing or unknowingly) as your identity constructors.

However, we are also unable to self-identify and self-define when we are not self-aware. Self-awareness is knowing who we are! It is knowing and owning who we are. Therein lies the real work because some of us would rather do anything else than face ourselves. We will find any and everything else way more interesting than getting to really know ourselves. What we want, what we don't want, what gives us pleasure, what makes us think but on top of all that WHO WE ARE. We define ourselves as the roles that were assigned to us based on the types of relationships we are in. I am that person's wife, or that one's daughter, or those children's mother, that one's sister, but who are we when we are not in those relationships? Who are we to ourselves? Let me tell you, some of us are nothing to ourselves and everything to everyone else. It was a lengthy journey for me to undergo the process of self-discovery and self-recognition. I had to learn through unlearning who I truly was and begin to walk in the truth of who I am. I had to leave the country! I was a 25-year-old closet case when I left South Africa, working extra hard to fit into the socially constructed roles that I was expected to fit into. I was constrained, boxed, and labeled.

I feel blessed to have been able to leave South Africa and introduce myself to myself. It is the most liberating thing I have ever done and, mind you, I have skinny-dipped before. However, you don't have to go teach English in South Korea or China to return to yourself. You can do it in the very space you are in. It's not easy but it is absolutely possible. What this process requires most is truth. In those silent moments where you are by yourself, in your thoughts, who are you? What do you want? What are your desires? Who are you when you are alone? Some of us have practiced silencing those voices even when we are alone. We have become quite exceptional at hiding that we even hide from ourselves. The masks we wear have layers upon layers, onions ain't got shit on us. We are different people in our different circles of influence. Our masks have become our identities. I was this person, I knew exactly which Khanyisa a situation called for and I presented her to perfection. You can imagine how grueling it was at times, and sometimes it still is, to peel through each layer to get to my core.

Society constructs their beliefs about who and what we will be; our job is to follow through with their preconceived ideas about our existence. We have to remember though that "society" is people. It is human beings, like you and me, trying to figure out this thing called life. In my culture (another man-made concept), girl children are raised to be mothers and wives. I was ready to be both by the age of nineteen. I started cooking for my family at the age of ten years old and doing laundry a few years before that. My family valued education but, when it came to choosing my career, my mother was front and center of that decision. She believed I possessed a strong sense of curiosity, leading her to narrow down my potential career choices to two: journalist or lawyer. I am neither, thank God! My grandmother was told that IT was the best career choice for her youngest son and that's what he was to study.

In his TED talk, Sir Ken Robinson talks about two different types of people: those who don't enjoy what they do, they simply do it for survival and wait for the weekend versus those who absolutely love what they do and it isn't what they do, it is who they are. Their work speaks to their true authentic selves. Sir Ken Robinson continues to speak about how education

"dislocates people from their natural talents. Human resources are like natural resources; they are often buried deep. You have to go looking for them, they are not just laying around on the surface. You have to create

the circumstances where they show themselves. And you might imagine
that education is the way that happens but too often it's not".

This rings true for my uncle and I imagine a lot of other people.
Sadly for some people, even though their talents were as obvious as the
color of the sky on a cloudless day; the circumstances created around
them buried those talents.

When my best friend told me about how much her younger sister
was struggling at school, especially with mathematics, I asked her what
her sister was good at. She said everything she could do with her hands
and long-distance running. At this point, my best friend had spent a
considerable amount of money on private tutoring in Johannesburg
making sure her sister followed in her footsteps. She was a mathematical
genius who completed her computer science degree in record time.

"Did you ask her what she wants to do?" a peculiar question indeed.

"Yes, but who cares, she needs to pass her matrix (grade 12)" she
replied, perplexed that I'd even ask such a ridiculous question.

"What did she say?"

"She said she wants to be a sound system engineer/DJ."

"Does she need an A in mathematics for that?"

"No."

I saw a lot of my peers when I was in University struggling, studying
courses that they knew nothing about and had zero passion for, because
they were never asked what they wanted and some were too scared to
say. That's not living. That's not being alive. There is a saying in my
language, isiXhosa "usana olungakhaliyo lufela embelwekini" (a baby
that doesn't cry dies at birth). Culture, society, and the education system
work hand-in-hand to stifle our creativity and silence our passions. How
many of us have, in a sense, died? We have died because we are not living
in our truth; we are living versions of ourselves that were not created by
us. All I heard throughout my schooling career was "education is the key
to success." I couldn't tell you how many times I heard that. Even
Nelson Mandela said it and, if Nelson said it, it must be true! How
many of us are sitting with degrees that we do not use? Paying student
loans that we will probably die never having finished paying? We are like
slaves to other people's dreams, expectations and visions of who we

should be. True living, not surviving, is expressed through demanding autonomy. Autonomy is the right to govern oneself, basically laying down the law for your own life. I say rule your castle with the ferocity of every Queen and King who has ever lived. Captain your ship. Create your canvas. LIVE.

You don't have to guess what happened to Anele. I'll tell you, he failed. Anele was set up to fail. Anele set himself up to fail. After a year of "trying," he came back home because it was too "hard." He lamented that the course was impossible if you didn't have a computer or couldn't afford expensive books. What a flawless justification coming from a gentleman who relied on the earnings of a prison cook to support his college education! Despite being impeccable, it remains merely an excuse. Numerous anecdotes exist of individuals in identical circumstances who successfully completed their academic degrees. Anele had taken up drinking in Pretoria. A lot of the money he was to use for making copies of the text books went into buying alcohol for him and his friends. He and my older cousin went to the same college; my cousin snitched. This is what happens when there is no passion and/or no motivation.

Let's take a moment to imagine what my uncle's life would have been like had he been allowed to be captain of his ship. If his talents were treated as resources and pure genius instead of distractions. What would have happened to Anele if he dared to follow his passions, chase after his dreams and see the blessing in his talents? He would have been one of the greatest boxing legends of our time. Honestly, he would have been whatever the fuck he chose and would have been excellent at it. I know he would have been exceptional at the sports he loved because he was great at all of them. Anele would have been an international sensation. I picture him in a big house in Johannesburg; that's where everyone goes when they "make it." They leave the villages for the glimmering lights of Johannesburg or the mother city, Cape Town. At 45 years old now, Anele would be a loving husband, a responsible father and probably retired, but coaching. He would have been loving because he would have been happy.

When we are living the lives we have chosen, lives that are in full alignment with who we are, we are more loving and full of joy. Have you ever met anyone who truly loved what they do; how much joy do they exude? They don't wake up grumpy, go to work grumpy, come home grumpy like the majority of the world. They are light on their feet, with big smiles and open hearts. It doesn't matter if what they do is challenging, no, they are joyous because it is who they are. Anele would have been one of those people had he continued on his chosen path.

Now let's do a quick "where are they now" like they do on the Oprah Winfrey show. Anele still lives in Cala, a small town. He is still a University drop out (I guess that never changes unless you go back to University and complete your education). A few things have changed; he is now a father of five and is rocking that dad bod. Four from two different women and one from his current wife. What was once a handsome face is now covered in scars from bar fights and his two front teeth are missing. He is an alcoholic who struggles to hold down a job and the only reason he still has one is because the town is so small that, when he fucks up, my grandmother gets called in and Anele is given another chance. He is still a child, an infant man still depending on his mother to give him direction. You can see him shadow box sometimes when he is drunk, singing "val'umnyango angabaleki." It is as if he has moments where he remembers who he truly is.

Let's take a moment and look at you now. Grab your pen and let's get to workin'.

1. Write down what you are doing with your life now (your job, what you are studying if you are a student).

_____

_____

_____

_____

_____

_____

_____

_____

_____

_____

_____

_____

_____

_____

_____

_____

_____

_____

_____

_____

_____

_____

_____

_____

_____

_____

_____

_____

_____

_____

2. Write down five things you love about your career choice and five things you wish would change.

_____

_____

_____

_____

_____

_____

_____

_____

_____

_____

_____

_____

_____

_____

_____

_____

_____

_____

_____

_____

_____

_____

_____

_____

_____

_____

_____

_____

_____

_____

_____

_____

_____

_____

3. If you were not in this career, what would you be doing?

_____
_____
_____
_____
_____
_____
_____
_____
_____
_____
_____
_____
_____
_____
_____
_____
_____
_____
_____
_____
_____
_____
_____
_____
_____
_____
_____
_____
_____
_____
_____
_____
_____
_____

4. Why are you not doing it?

_____
_____
_____
_____
_____
_____
_____
_____
_____
_____
_____
_____
_____
_____
_____
_____
_____
_____
_____
_____
_____
_____
_____
_____
_____
_____
_____
_____

5. On a scale of 1-10, how content are you with your life and why?

_____

_____

_____

_____

_____

_____

_____

_____

_____

_____

_____

_____

_____

_____

_____

_____

_____

_____

_____

_____

_____

_____

_____

_____

_____

_____

_____

_____

_____

_____

_____

_____

When you can honestly answer these questions and at the end you feel, yeah I am doing exactly what I should be in my life, then great! Keep doing it. But if you know that something is lacking, something just doesn't feel right, something is not **clicking** - then perhaps you need to be in *intensional pursuit* of what will set your soul on fire. For me, writing this book, and encouraging you to LIVE, is what sets my soul on fire. What brings me joy is talking to a client and they tell me that they have made a leap in their lives, or they have finally made that decision they were scared to make, that is what gives me joy. Find the thing for you.

Start by making a list of the things that you love to do, and then make a list of the things you enjoy doing. When you look at the lists, find the things that coincide with each other and see how they can become what you do in your life. We want a purpose to come from a deep inner voice, a loud, deep voice that says "this is what you should do with your life." But I believe that it is much simpler than that. It is in the things that we do daily, the things that we love and we can share with others. Do not look further than yourself; it is right there, in you.

LIVE, PASSIONATELY.

Two

Live, Bravely

"True freedom is the capacity for acting according to one's true character, to be altogether one's self, to be self-determined and not subject to outside coercion."

— Corliss Lamont, American philosopher and political activist

My family has two sets of plates, two sets of cutlery, two sets of pots and pans, basically two sets of everything a household needs. The old sets, the ones with chipped glass on the sides, the broken mug handles and burned pot bottoms, are the ones we use daily. We save the better sets for special events where we will have people coming over. Those are for funerals, traditional ceremonies and the random visit from the church group. We have a special place for that special set for those special people who visit us on those special events. Once chipped or misused, the special set is put with the plates we use daily and when there is money, a new special set is bought for the special people, who are not us.

We used these new plates, pots and cutlery to impress people - the special people who come to all the special events. We would spend every single cent we had to make sure their tea had milk, their lunch had meat and their plates were unchipped. We ate last when they were there, making sure that their bellies were full before we would serve ourselves. We wanted them to know that they mattered more than us. You must be thinking that my family wanted to show respect and honor their guests. In part, I agree with that. However, a big part of that was our need to make sure that their opinion of us when they left was a positive one. I don't even know who these people were, it was just "abantu"- people.

"Bazothini abantu" (What will people say).

This was and is still my family mantra. It was and sometimes, more times than I'd like to admit, **is** my personal mantra. My grandmother has buried six out of her ten children, six! She called me for some counseling when her favorite son died, her heart broken into a thousand pieces. She confessed to not wanting to cry too much because she feared what people would say about her faith in God if she cried "too much."

She said, "When I wouldn't stop crying after I heard the news, my neighbors said 'no Mamzima, it's going to start looking like you don't trust God' and that made me stop because I trust God."

She also confessed to wondering what people were saying about her children dying. I knew what she was alluding to when she shared this concern. She was afraid that people would think she was a witch. This is the trauma that awaits Black women in the villages as they age, being labeled a witch. I, on the other hand, am a regular visitor at the no fucks to give club. This is how I tried to get her to join the club:

"Where were people when your children were sick and you had to nurse them?" I asked

"Nowhere, I was alone." she replied with her voice shaking.

"Where are people now, in your grief?"

"I am still alone."

"Then why do you care so much about what they think of you?"

This last question was met with silence. I couldn't believe that my grandmother, in her eighties, was still so concerned about people's opinions. I had imagined that we grow out of that, that we reach an age where we don't give a damn about what people think of us. I was looking forward to getting to an age where I didn't care about what people thought. I was convinced that eighty is definitely that age, but the queen of my heart proved me wrong.

Here was the bravest woman I know, stifling her grief out of the fear of what people thought of her. I am no longer a practicing Christian but I knew enough scripture to help my grandmother. That's the language she speaks best, "**Christianese**", and I know quite a bit of it. So, when I didn't know what to say to her anymore, I quoted David in the book of Psalms.

"Against You, You only, I have sinned and done what is evil in Your sight, So that You are justified when You speak and blameless when You judge." Psalm 51:4

My grandmother knew what I was trying to say to her through these words. She knew that I was reminding her that even David, in his darkest of times, had to remind himself that his relationship was with God alone. David knew that he was being judged by others for what he had done - I think this is when he killed that woman's husband. So, in his prayer, David decided to focus on what truly mattered to him. God. His relationship with Him and in this scripture, David releases himself from the chains of people's opinions. He frees himself, not from accountability for his sin, but from being a prisoner of what other people thought of him. Our relentless concern about "what other people think of us" shackles us to a life of being prisoners of their imagined opinions of us.

I asked my ex-girlfriend to "table our breakup" three times. The first time she wrote me a letter. We were sitting at our favorite restaurant. They were playing the first song I'd ever sung to her; "Sorry" by Tracy Chapman, and she was writing me a breakup letter. She asked that I give her a few minutes while she wrote it as she needed to "choose her words wisely." She handed it to me when she was done, acknowledging the fact that our song was playing. I was hoping the song would remind her of... "Us." It didn't. I read through it and asked her to table it. The second time was at 2 a.m., during a heated fight over her infidelity, she wrote yet another breakup letter. I don't remember everything that was in that letter but the words "I feel trapped" and "I love you but I'm not in love with you" will never leave my memory. Again, I asked for this breakup to be tabled. The last breakup was said using words, well words from the mouth. I said, "Give it a week and let's see."

I don't even know what the fuck that means now - "table a breakup." I stayed three months longer after that. Enduring a series of falsehoods and a lack of respect has been my unfortunate experience, primarily driven by my overwhelming fear of potential public reactions in the event of our separation. We'd been together for seven years, had people calling us #couplegoals and I loved that. Our relationship was a persona of its own, a massive identifier of who I was and the thought of it ending was unbearable. What would people think of me? I imagined my old Christian friends laughing at me that my girlfriend cheated on me with a man. I could hear them, talking about how that was bound to happen because being a homosexual was a sin. I also imagined our friends who loved us feeling sad and upset that we had broken up. I agonized at the thought of our followers on social media throwing an emotional fit over their "favorite couple" breaking up.

I stayed in a relationship with someone who begged me to let them go. Someone who was clear that she didn't want to be with me anymore but I instead turned around and begged them to stay. Say it with me now: ***What will people say?*** After my heart couldn't handle the pain anymore, this is what I told myself. "People" are not in this. They are not in this house with someone who doesn't even look like the person they fell in love with. They are not experiencing this pain that feels like a constant gut punch. They are not the ones whose "I love yous" are met with silence. I reminded myself that all of this shit was happening to me, and me alone. This thought process gave me the strength I needed to let her go and in doing so, I set myself free. All I had to deal with was myself, my broken heart, but the thought of people's opinions was no longer a factor in how I was going to deal with the breakup. There were no fucking people!

I attended a friend's wedding a few years ago. Now, Black people in South Africa have no respect for invitations, so, if you invite one person, they could potentially show up with four plus ones! Your catered wedding, which you had planned for your one hundred closest friends and family, may end up being a big wedding with well over two hundred people. This was my friend's wedding, a whole village feast. She glowed in her white wedding dress, her bridesmaids looked stunning in their peach dresses while the groom and his groomsmen looked dashing in their suits and matching peach ties. This was the white wedding.

They then had to throw a "traditional wedding" the day after the white wedding. All their outfits were new, more food was served and plenty more alcohol was drunk. I didn't know how deep the financial hole was that my friend and her husband began their new lives with until they confessed that they were still paying for the wedding three years into their marriage.

"Our dream is to travel, in a perfect world, we would have gotten married at a courthouse and used that money to travel for a few months," she said regretfully.

"Why didn't you?" I asked.

"Our families wanted us to have the wedding. Especially my mom, she always wonders about what people will say if we do things differently."

"What did your family, especially your mom, help with at the wedding?"

"Nothing, we paid for the whole thing ourselves."

Not only did my friends not fulfill their dream of traveling together, but they were in a lot of debt because they cared so much about "what people would say" if they went to the magistrate's court and got married. If they had used their hard-earned money to do something that *they* wanted to do. They have sacrificed what they truly desire for their lives to please people. How often do we all do this: abandon ourselves out of the fear of other people's opinions on how we choose to live our lives? We value people's opinions about our lives way more than we value our own.

This is the truth that I know about "people" - brace yourself, this is the good stuff. "People" *don't give a shit*. Sit with that for a second. "People" don't give a flying fuck about what happens to you, how you feel, how the events in YOUR life affect you. Here's why; "people" are busy trying to sort their own shit out. They are absorbed in themselves and when they lift their heads for a split second, it's not that they care, they need to numb their pain with yours. Let's think about this. People who have time to give an opinion on your life are not taking the time to look at themselves. Your life's mess is a welcome diversion from their own. Knowing this truth has made my life a little bit easier and my fuck giving a lot less.

Maybe caring so much about what people say makes us feel special. We feel like we matter enough for someone to insert their opinions on the most personal parts of our lives, like our relationships, our careers, and our faith. Maybe it stems from our need to be loved and accepted. We learn from a very young age to give people access to these intimate parts of ourselves. We are made to believe that their opinions are from a place of love. Perhaps they are. Nonetheless, if people have such an impact on our lives, we are not truly living. We have given them power over us. We have shackled ourselves with chains of people's opinions. We have got to liberate ourselves!

In her book, *The Life-Fhanging Magic of Not Giving a Fuck,* Sarah Knight talks about the power of not giving a fuck. No, this doesn't mean you have to be a reckless human being who doesn't give a shit about anything, but rather a call to free yourself from a life lived with too many fucks given. She talks about a "fucks bank," where you prioritize your fucks. For example, I give a fuck if my girlfriend likes my cologne, she has to smell it, but I don't give a fuck about what a distant cousin thinks about my life. It's so simple! It's also very difficult to practice.

I have a quick confession to make: I am currently writing this chapter in the cozy confines of our studio apartment, which my girlfriend and I share. I have been in Australia for almost eight months now and being on a student visa has limited my job options. I have been working as a waitress for a while and now, well now I'm just not working. I haven't told my family because I am scared of what they will say. I keep thinking of how what I am doing, or not doing, is failing them. I am also someone who is very active on social media but I haven't posted about my current predicament. I am scared of what people will say. How I went from owning businesses in the Philippines to cleaning up half-eaten avocado toasts and taking orders from people much younger than me. I don't have it all figured out yet or I have, but like I said, it is difficult to practice.

I'm a big believer in "faking it 'till you make it." It works most of the time, even Brene Brown agrees. What if you started by saying it, just say you don't care what people think about you. Claim this freedom until you can experience it. Tell yourself that your life is yours and yours alone. There are people whom you invite to share in it but ultimately, it is yours.

Grab that pen and answer these questions for me!

~

1. How would this less fucks given attitude change the way you make decisions?

_____

_____

_____

_____

_____

_____

_____

_____

_____

_____

_____

_____

_____

_____

_____

_____

_____

_____

_____

_____

_____

_____

_____

_____

_____

_____

_____

2. How would the way you interact with the world change?

_____
_____
_____
_____
_____
_____
_____
_____
_____
_____
_____
_____
_____
_____
_____
_____
_____
_____
_____
_____
_____
_____
_____
_____
_____
_____
_____
_____
_____
_____
_____
_____
_____

3. What freedom will you experience when you let go of the fear of people's opinions?

_____

_____

_____

_____

_____

_____

_____

_____

_____

_____

_____

_____

_____

_____

_____

_____

_____

_____

_____

_____

_____

_____

_____

_____

_____

_____

_____

_____

This is what I imagine for you. Freedom. Complete, unhinged, uninhibited, unrestrained, freedom. Freedom to be WHO and WHAT you are here to be. Freedom to make mistakes, freedom to fail, freedom to choose. Freedom to disappoint people, freedom to maybe disappoint yourself at times. Freedom to LIVE. To Thrive. Freedom to be in the fullest expression of yourself. Once you let go of this fear, you will release yourself! Baby, I want this freedom for you. I hope you want it for yourself too. You can do this. You can LIVE.

LIVE, BRAVELY

THREE
LIVE, OPENLY

"Spirituality speaks from the soul. Religion speaks from the mind."

— RAINN WILSON, AMERICAN ACTOR, WRITER, AND
DIRECTOR

My grandfather was a priest in a small church called The Bantu Church of Christ (BCC); he was the head priest of the branch in Cala. BCC is an extension of the orthodox Seventh Day Adventist Church but as all things go, each has an issue with the other although they are 100% the same thing. We attended church every Saturday: morning service at 11am and evening service at 3pm, just like Seventh Day Adventists. We stopped using heat on Friday afternoons, didn't eat pork, didn't wear pants, didn't wear makeup (I was too young anyway) but you get the point. My grandfather's church was all about the rules! What I can think of as a main distinguishing factor is that Seventh Day Adventists tended to have nicer churches, and they all dressed very nicely. The women did wear makeup and painted their nails. My grandfather's church also totally missed the boat on how much money churches can accumulate. You know how some churches have bags for collecting money at every single service? Well, my grandfather used small plates, the ones used to put your tea cup on. Perhaps it's true that the Lord does give according to your expectations.

My tall, handsome, asthmatic grandfather was not much of a talker, let alone a charismatic preacher. His long silver beard was a perfect accessory to his all-black priest uniform - the long black gown, his black shirt with a white color and a gray suit. I remember his husky voice during songs and him quietly praying with one knee on the ground. I loved going to church with my grandfather; he always had a free hand to hold mine and candy for whenever I needed one. I was only nine years old when I watched my grandfather die in his garden, and I have forgotten a lot of what he used to preach about. What I do remember was the simplicity of his teaching, mostly because my grandmother would always reiterate them after his passing. She would tell me about his favorite scriptures "honor your father and mother so that your days may be lengthened" and "spare the rod, spoil the child." These are scriptures she would recall when I was in trouble or in defiance of her. You can see why, right? They are very effective.

There was a marriage of church and tradition in my grandfather's house. He was a Christian priest who performed traditional ancestral ceremonies. It was seamless to him, his way of marrying the two. He would preach a fiery sermon about Jesus on Saturday and slaughter a goat as an offering for the ancestors on Sunday. He knew himself to be a Xhosa man who was a Christian. Holding both identities was not a struggle for him. Every slaughtered goat was an offering to the ancestors and every church song sung was worship to God.

This was my life as well when I lived with him. I was as attached to his Christianity as I was to his traditions. I would pop a squat next to him as he passed around the traditional beer "umqombothi" from his mouth, skipping me of course, to the next man in the circle. I was still young enough to be allowed to sit with the men. When he died, the traditions took a back seat and Christianity drove the spiritual bus in our home. My grandmother would do a small traditional ceremony here and there but these became less and less with time. The traditional practices completely died down when my mother joined a Pentecostal church and took us (me and my brothers) with her. This is one of those non-denominational, tongue-speaking, demon-basting and difference-hating types of churches. This is where I learnt to divorce traditional ceremonies and keep my religion. We were taught that the two simply could not work together, and traditional or cultural practices were defined as demonic.

"Jesus already died for your sins, why do you need to slaughter goats as an offering?" This would be preached at the pulpit and my mother and I would shout one of the loudest "amens."

I bought into this preaching all through high school and early years of University. I loved the idea of a God who loved me so intensely and passionately that He was jealous *for* me. He, God, was jealous ***for*** me. Note: not jealous of me. He didn't want me to believe in anything else but Him, or love anything else but Him. I was wanted by God. This is what you get from being raised by your grandparents, while your parents are still alive but not in your life. You cling to whatever love comes your way and I honestly was lucky. I clung to a less (physically) destructive love but (emotionally) it broke me into a million pieces. I also basked in the loving community that the church created for me. I was all about Church! Well, this is until I realized that church wasn't all about me. It is soul-sucking to love something that you know will not love you back when it finds out who you truly are.

I knew I was gay since I was in high school and I believed I would go to hell for it. The fear of hell, the shame of being found out and being isolated kept me in the closet for a really long time. The illusion of church folk is in their sense of self-righteousness - that how they CHOOSE to live is the "right way to live." Let's settle this real quick, your religion is a choice; nothing less and nothing more. Embedded in this self-righteousness is the overarching superiority complex. Being the ones entrusted with all the "spiritual truths" and thus making them the defenders of God. Their collective spiritual experience serves as an invasion of others' personal lives. Think about the idea of confession. Confessing your sins to each other in order to find forgiveness. It felt as if my life was to be experienced by my church constituents and passing judgment on each other was not only permitted but also expected. Let me share this with you from *A Course In Miracles*; this changed my life!

"God does not forgive, because God does not condemn."

We are therefore not seeking God's forgiveness but that of ourselves and those who have condemned us.

I still carry some guilt for how I treated people when I was a born-again Christian. Nothing I did was Christ-like! I was the Christian Gandhi spoke of when he said "I love your Christ but dislike your Christians." In his book, *God is not a Christian*, Archbishop Desmond Tutu addresses these Christian "truths" as false. He eloquently explains that no religion has a monopoly on God. He beckons us to think about the Old Testament dudes who were not Christians; is Moses in hell? How about David, is he in the fiery flames experiencing eternal damnation? Let's bring it a little closer to our time. Is Ghandi in hell? What about all the kind, loving, and amazing human beings who were not Christians: are their souls being tortured because they were not Christians?

Although a born again Christian, my mother would always caution me against believing that there was only one way to pray, worship and connect with God. She strongly rejected the negative view our church had of Catholicism and other Christian denominations. She would always say "He has to hear all of us, we are all His. Can you imagine how bored He would be if we ALL prayed the same way?" I took her belief even further when I lived in Malaysia, a predominantly Muslim country. My roommates were practicing Muslims who prayed five times a day, didn't eat pork, covered their hair and beat themselves up for having had premarital sex. Although there are major differences in the theology of both religions, the similarities were hard to miss. My one roommate couldn't hide the shame and guilt she bore for breaking her virginity. While on the other hand, my other roommate handled herself with the innocence of a Christian virgin.

When I finally got the courage to break free from church dogma, I did. But, I did miss it. I missed the songs, the community and knowing that God was listening. Although I was not a Christian, I was never an atheist. I held onto the belief of a higher power, the existence of something miraculous and divine. I had seen and experienced so many unexplainable things in church that I knew saying "there is no God" would not be true for me. From the woman who was in a wheelchair but began to walk when the pastor laid hands on her and prayed to the testimonies of regular people who were experiencing miracles in their lives. Do not get me started on the exorcism that I saw; I saw so many that I could also tell when someone was faking.

Pentecostal churches in South Africa love having "tent conferences". These are essentially church services that run every day for a week and are held in a big white tent. The tent is of course bigger than the church building and can hold a lot more people. These tent conferences are also filled with spiritual wonders and miracles - from people getting out of wheelchairs to demons living in people's bodies. One holy ghost-filled night, a girl started screaming and shaking as if Satan himself had inhabited her body. She threw herself on chairs, safely landing in the arms of the strong male ushers behind her. I watched the main pastor that night tell her, "If you don't stop faking, I will slap you across the face." Satan left her the same way he entered - through the attention-seeking hole. She fell silent, collected herself and took a seat at the back.

As much as there were fake ones, I really believe that some were also real. I once saw a grown man scale the side of a church wall like a snake. He just slithered, a whole man turned into a crawling animal. It took almost an hour and all the men in the church to get him down and finally exorcize the "snake animal spirit" that was controlling him. I'm not one to argue about the technicalities of what went on at these. I don't know if some of these were paid actors as the media suggests, but I had personal moments myself. My most vivid memory was when I went to a Benny Hinn conference with my mother. He asked the whole church to stand as he could feel the presence of God and we needed to show reverence. I decided that I was done standing for the night and just sat. He repeated the instruction about three times until he said "young lady, you will respect the presence of God and stand." I still get chills thinking about this. I got up and then he continued. This is particularly divine to me because I was way far back for Benny to see me, but not far enough for God.

Some bible verses resonated with my soul, like the story of the woman with the issue of blood who touched Jesus' hem. I LOVE that story; maybe it was the outcast who got to touch Jesus passing all the "worthy" ones around her, and Jesus' acceptance of her. I love the underdogs. Those who are not seduced by what is popular but follow their heart's longing. I love them, and I envy them. Their bravery in resisting sameness but cling to what it is that makes them...them.

I would always imagine this scene: this woman in her raggedy clothes, crawling in pain, onlookers pinching their nostrils and her determination to "just touch the hem of his garment" and she does! She does and she finds healing. Not only does she find healing but she receives grace.

I also love the story of the prostitute who washed Jesus' feet. Another outcast, probably considered the lowest of the low but somehow gets to kneel before Jesus, washes his feet with oil and wipes them with her hair. All sounds sexy hey! I love this one more because this woman is told to leave, but Jesus says "no, let her stay and wash my feet." This story makes me feel that Jesus loves the underdog as much as I do. That He is not impressed by perfectionists and "holier than thous" but is drawn to those deemed unworthy. I love this Jesus who touches dirty women and gets his feet washed by prostitutes.

And then there is Paul. Paul and I would have had some serious debates if we would have met, but ohhh give me 1 Corinthians 13 every damn day and I swoon.

> *"4 Love is patient, love is kind. It does not envy, it does not boast, it is not proud. 5 It does not dishonor others, it is not self-seeking, it is not easily angered, it keeps no record of wrongs. 6 Love does not delight in evil but rejoices with the truth. 7 It always protects, always trusts, always hopes, always perseveres." 1 Corinthians 4-7.*

In all of these, all these miracles, these wonders, I didn't stop feeling unloved by God and ultimately church folk and their preaching made me feel like people like me don't belong to God. To me, I was just never gonna be good enough; gay and Christian was not an acceptable combo. I left but something inside me MISSED divine presence. No matter how much I ignored it, I missed knowing that God had me in the palm of His hands. I searched for it somewhere else, somewhere outside the collective spirituality of institutionalized religions and I found it. I found it outside church hallways and Tuesday Bible Study Groups. I found it in what I define as spirituality; a PERSONAL experience of divine presence.

Let me explain! My first step was opening up to the idea that perhaps there is more than just one way to God. I can hear the screams of Christians as I write this - "blasphemy!" This began with me living in different parts of the world and being friends with people who were of different religions. These were - well are, they're not dead, - good people. They were not good because they were Muslims, they were good because they were people who had good hearts and happened to be Muslims. These people opened their homes to me, fed me, held me when I felt down and simply cared for a stranger. To them, my religion was a non-factor, all they saw was my humanity.

Then in that book by Archbishop Tutu I mentioned earlier, he posed a question that I could not ignore. The Arch writes "if we are saying only Christians go to heaven, the men in the Old Testament were not Christians. Are we to believe that they went to hell? Are we saying that God is so petty that He would send good, kind, loving people to hell just because they were not Christians?" I can't believe that. I can't believe that a loving God is going to send me to hell for the sin of *loving* a woman. I also can't believe a loving God created hell to send his children who don't love him. Like what the actual f!? The narcissism and pettiness of the Christian God are honestly not attractive.

I personally don't identify with any religious group. I think the idea that we have to even put our religion when filling out forms is beyond ludicrous. Why does it even matter!? Although not religious, I am very spiritual. My spirituality has allowed me to find the beauty in all religious texts. A monk friend of mine told me that I was a *NONE*; nothing but everything. I want to be able to experience divinity in as many different ways as I can. I am open to every single spiritual practice there is - note that I said spiritual and not religious. You will find me barefoot in a forest, singing around a fire with witches, or sitting cross-legged in a temple meditating with monks, and once in a while, you will find me with my hands lifted high singing hallelujah with Christians (at an all-inclusive church - obviously).

Living is having the freedom to choose and yes, that includes choosing what spiritual path you want to undertake - should you decide that it is an experience you want to have. It is not something that we are "born with" although it is most certainly something you are "born into." It is most likely that you would have been a Muslim had you been born in the Middle East or a Jew if you were from Israel. Spirituality is a personal journey; it is your soul's longing for something outside of what we can see and something un-intangible. Spirituality is also knowing that you do not get to dictate what others do with their journey. One of my biggest regrets in life is condemning people who lived differently from me when I was a Christian. I feel mortified when I think of the hate that came out of my mouth in the name of a loving God. It is also no one's business, not even your parents', if you decide that none of it works for you. This life is yours to LIVE.

I want you to take stock of your own spiritual journey, go grab your pen!

~

1. What is my spiritual practice?

_____
_____
_____
_____
_____
_____
_____
_____
_____
_____
_____
_____
_____
_____
_____
_____
_____
_____
_____
_____
_____
_____
_____
_____
_____
_____
_____
_____
_____
_____

2. How does my spirituality bring me joy?

_____
_____
_____
_____
_____
_____
_____
_____
_____
_____
_____
_____
_____
_____
_____
_____
_____
_____
_____
_____
_____
_____
_____
_____
_____
_____
_____
_____
_____
_____

3. How do I lean into my spirituality in challenging times?

_____
_____
_____
_____
_____
_____
_____
_____
_____
_____
_____
_____
_____
_____
_____
_____
_____
_____
_____
_____
_____
_____
_____
_____
_____
_____
_____
_____
_____
_____
_____
_____
_____

Imagine this scenario for a moment: residing in a world where one's religious or spiritual choices are deeply personal and individualistic. How we choose to pray or not pray is not an offense to anyone but a personal experience. A world where Christian and Muslim parents don't disown their children for being gay because "that goes against their religion", where schools allow the expression of every religion/spiritual practice and not just Christianity. A world where not one more war is fought in the name of religion or not one more old woman is killed under suspicion of being a witch because someone caught her burning sage at three in the morning. I will never ever say there should be no religion, that is not for me to say, but I will say that it doesn't need to be ugly and it definitely doesn't need to be forced down other people's throats. Even Paul agrees when he writes ***"work out your OWN salvation with fear and trembling."***

LIVE, OPENLY

FOUR
LIVE, FREELY

"The chief part of a person's happiness consists of pleasure."

— THOMAS MORE, BRITISH PHILOSOPHER

The girl who brought pornography magazines to school when I was in grade seven was the granddaughter of a priest at the Methodist church. She was a year older than me and ten years ahead when it came to sex. She always had a group of students around her desk, giggling as they tried to look inconspicuous. Nontlantla was her name - it means lucky in Xhosa. Nontlantla reveled in the attention that her porno magazines brought her. Before this, Nontlantla was known for her stinky armpits - I know, cruel! She was isolated, the other girls would gossip about her and a few bold mean girls would pinch their nostrils when she walked by. Not to sound holier than thou, but I wasn't one of Nontlantla's torturers, not because of anything other than the fact that she and I were in the same boat. I too was an easy target for bullies, my lunch box was forcefully shared between me and some older boys in class, and I too was laughed at for my torn-up school uniform that was handed down to me by my cousin. Nontlantla and I had a lot in common, except for the stinky armpits - my grandmother would never allow that to happen.

Nontlantla's status improved the moment she started smuggling those magazines to school. She was this short little girl carrying a backpack too heavy for her stature because of her "product." We would all circle around her every time there was no teacher in the classroom and then scatter like cockroaches running from the light when one walked in. Nontlantla had a week of badassery until a teacher walked in on us with our eyes glued to the magazine - we were all not so lucky that day but she was the most unlucky one. Sir Puza, our Math's teacher who was known for his meanness and quickness to use the switch, strutted into the classroom ready to deal with us. He sternly demanded that we bring it over to him, snitch on the culprit - which wasn't that hard to do and we all got punished. Her fame was short-lived but I couldn't unsee what I saw in those magazines.

Sir Puza didn't report us to the principal nor to our parents. He simply beat the shit out of us and confiscated those "disgusting" magazines. He rolled up all four magazines, threw them in a plastic bag and walked out as though he was going to the trash can. We didn't SEE him trash them. I bet you're thinking what I'm thinking... he took them for his own collection. Don't get me wrong, I am glad he didn't tell my grandmother, his lashes on the hand would have been minuscule compared to what she would have done to my inner thighs. However, his rage and the words he used began the planting of the seed of the disgusting act that is sex. It also made me very curious. Isn't that how that always works? Everything that is considered taboo creates a sense of curiosity. This is what that reaction did to me. Not that I wanted to have sex, no, but I wanted to look at it.

I have never wondered where Nontlantla got those magazines, just like I didn't wonder where my cousin got his "blue movies." Blue movies were after Nontlantla, maybe about six months after. My aunt had a VCR at her house and somehow, my cousin got his hands on some hardcore pornography tapes. All our friends would congregate around my aunt's small TV while she was at work or church or the store and watch. I honestly don't know where she would go long enough for us to watch pornography in her one-bedroom apartment for an entire hour. My cousin was much older than me; he had to know that I shouldn't have been in that room but there I was, eyes glued to the screen, watching White people moan and grind on each other. Sex was not only disgusting now, it was also racial. All the magazines had White people, so did the blue movies and most of the soap operas where the kissing was intense mostly had White actors.

I would always feel guilty after every blue movie session. I would walk to my grandmother's house and would want to gouge my eyes out. The guilt was real but it didn't outweigh the fear of my grandmother. The creativity in that woman's punishment is unmatched! She once took a teacup and sent it flying across one of my uncles' mouths. The two front teeth are still missing, serving as a reminder of the ferocity that is his mother. I kept my pornography watching a secret, my knowledge of the workings of SEX was only known to me and my cousins. These early years of exploration revealed sex to be disgusting, shameful (because what happens in porn is shameful) and is to be kept a secret. It was also the thing that White people did. All I saw in both the magazines and the blue movies were white, naked bodies.

Sex found me when I was ten years old. It came uninvited, invasive and aggressive. It still carried shame, guilt and silence. It found me during a big family event where we even had extended family members from out of town attending. My cousins and I were playing on one side of the yard, while the women cooked on the other side. The men must have finished slaughtering the sheep for the event; it's the only explanation that makes sense as to why my uncle was in his room by himself. He popped his head outside of the window as it faced the side of the yard we were playing on. He yelled out "Yiz'apha Khayisa" (come here Khanyisa). Nothing was unusual about this, my uncles used to call me and send me around all the time. They'd be sitting in the living room and would call me from wherever I was to send me to the kitchen for a glass of water. They'd also send me to the shops for cigarettes and beer - my town didn't care about age restrictions. Doing what I was accustomed to, I went to my uncle's bedroom but instead of being sent to buy or fetch him something, I was told to stay.

My uncle, lying on his back, instructed me to get in bed next to him. He motioned for me to lay on my back, next to him and rolled over to place his tall body on mine. I froze, I don't remember how long he laid on me. All I remember is the breathing, the sweating, the panting and his heavy body dropping on mine and he lay there, frozen. He finally revived his body, rolled off me and told me to go. Dazed, confused and scared, I put my underwear on and slowly began to reach for the door. Right when I was about to exit, Eric, my uncle, said "Don't tell anyone about this, okay, we will both be in trouble. No one needs to know, this is our little secret." Another sex-related secret. I kept walking, pained between my legs, a pain I had never experienced before. I didn't cry, I knew if I cried, I would have to say why and I would be in trouble. Instead, I went back to my cousins and did whatever it was that they were doing, forcing myself to forget about the pain between my legs. That was it, sex had touched me. Sex had found a way out of my mind and into my body — inhabiting all the parts of me. Sex didn't ask for any of these parts; not my mind and definitely not my body — it just took them. It didn't care that I wasn't ready to give.

I was in secondary school when the HIV/AIDS epidemic hit South Africa, forcing teachers to talk to us about sex. I can still feel my teacher's discomfort every time she would say "isondo" which means sex in Xhosa. The government realized that young kids needed to be taught about sex, specifically abstinence to help prevent the increasing spread of HIV. In its efforts, it invested a lot of money in programs that were geared toward teaching young learners about sex. These programs ranged from visitations from a group of people doing plays about sex, students asked to do plays about what they've learned about the disease, and introduction to condoms. We were young but we knew that HIV/AIDS was a sex disease.

Teachers were suddenly tasked with the enormous job of teaching young students about sex. EVERYONE was uncomfortable. We were all NOT okay. We, the students, came up with ways to ease the discomfort. We abbreviated SEX to *Science, English, Xhosa* and AIDS was *America's Idea to Destroy Sex*. What were we doing?! We were trying to find a way to ease into the conversation, to make it humorous and dismantle its power - the power it had to make everyone in the room fall into utter discomfort. Teachers did the best they could to teach us. They would talk about condoms, consent and then end with the much preferred form of protection - abstinence. They did the best they could to drill into our heads that the only way to not get AIDS was to abstain from sex. So, not only was sex disgusting and shameful but it could literally kill you.

When I became a born-again Christian at fourteen years old, sex was spoken of only in terms of its implications for those who have it outside of marriage. We were strongly encouraged to wait until we were married to avoid going to hell. Sex was reserved for one man and one woman when they joined each other in marriage. The Christian term for sex outside of marriage is *fornication*. Fornicators were going to hell, along with homosexuals, Muslims, atheists and Oprah. We were encouraged to only date when we were ready for marriage. It wasn't even called dating but rather "courtship." We were taught "holy" ways of courtship which ranged from supervised dates to minimizing physical contact. We were taught to look forward to being married as that is when we would partake in sex for the purpose of reproducing. Sex was for the purpose of making babies.

I tell you these tales of my beliefs around sex and pleasure because I'm not the only one whose mentality about sex was totally fucked. The messages I received about sex all formed my deep-seated beliefs about intercourse, intimacy and connection. Pornography, rape, and even church dogma, all formed the belief that sex was shameful. I was never taught about sex as intimacy between loving people or that it was a form of pleasure. Pleasure. A thing you enjoy doing. A thing that makes you feel good. A thing you can do to yourself, by yourself and with yourself. A thing you can do with one person, or more should you so choose and should they so agree. A thing that you, as a woman, can absolutely love and speak of and ask for. A thing you can do even if you don't want to have children, or can't have them.

Guilty Pleasures

How many of us feel guilty for doing and having things that we absolutely enjoy? It's not just sex, some of us subconsciously choose to live a life of poverty because we have negative beliefs about money. We are never taught about the joys that come with having money. We even feel guilty for admitting that we love money. There is so much shame and stigma around money - shame for having too much of it and shame for not having enough of it. We subconsciously and consciously deny ourselves things that we know we LOVE because of what we were raised to believe about them. Listen to the way in which people talk about money: "The love of money is the root of evil," "money doesn't grow on trees," "people who have a lot of money are bad." How can you attract something that you believe is evil? Why is it that society makes things that bring us pleasure, joy and fulfillment taboo?

It is as if we have convinced ourselves that our goal is to suffer so we can find eternal joy after we die. We are walking around trying to avoid having the very human experience that we are here to have. We have allowed outside influences to place rigid limitations on the experiences that we can have in our own lives. I say fuck that! LIVE! Do, have, eat, indulge in travel, and have all the experiences you want to have, just make sure you are not harming yourself or other people. I remember the time I had an orgy. Four women consensually enjoying each other's bodies. It was liberating. It was pleasurable. I was joyous. It was a big "fuck you" to every shameful belief I had about sex. It freed me. I call you to freedom!

I want you to think about your own relationship with pleasure, go grab your pen!

~

1. What are some of my negative beliefs about pleasure?

_____
_____
_____
_____
_____
_____
_____
_____
_____
_____
_____
_____
_____
_____
_____
_____
_____
_____
_____
_____
_____
_____
_____
_____
_____
_____
_____

2. How can I reframe those beliefs and allow myself intentional moments of being in pleasure?

_____
_____
_____
_____
_____
_____
_____
_____
_____
_____
_____
_____
_____
_____
_____
_____
_____
_____
_____
_____
_____
_____
_____
_____
_____
_____
_____
_____
_____
_____

3. Make a list of things that you do for pleasure and commit to doing one of them at least once a week.

_____

_____

_____

_____

_____

_____

_____

_____

_____

_____

_____

_____

_____

_____

_____

_____

_____

_____

_____

_____

_____

_____

_____

_____

_____

_____

_____

_____

_____

_____

_____

You know how this goes, let's do it, let's imagine what life would look like if we allowed ourselves pleasure. Imagine allowing yourself to be human, actually giving yourself permission to LIVE. Not just breathe, work, survive and die, but to actually LIVE. To honor all those things that are pleasurable to you. Imagine the joy you will experience when you unabashedly allow yourself the freedom to indulge in what feels good to you.

To try things, things that scare you and actually excite you when you think about them. How would it feel? No seriously - is it a threesome, is it sucking your partner's toes, is it a vacation, ice cream before dinner - whatever it is, imagine yourself doing it. Now do it. Go ahead, indulge, experience, try, LIVE.

LIVE, FREELY

FIVE

LIVE, RESPONSIBLY

"Responsibility breeds empowerment."

— KHANYISA MNYAKA

My grandparents raised eight children in a two-room house. Note that I didn't say "bedroom" but room. The house had eight walls. The kitchen where they cooked and the room where they slept. My grandparents shared their bed with whoever was the youngest, and the rest slept on the floor. They had three girls and five boys. I should add myself as the ninth because I was also raised by my grandparents. They raised me as their youngest child. However, when I was thirteen years old I found out that I wasn't theirs. Let me give you a bit of background on who these people were, how they met and how they ended up with eight children, in the small town of Cala. My grandfather was the fifth of nine boys and one girl from his parents. He was also the most handsome. This is not bias, this is what I was told. He was a carpenter, which makes sense that in his old age, he was a priest. (You know, Jesus was a carpenter and my grandfather - a carpenter turned priest). Legend and by legend I mean my aunts and uncles, say that my grandfather had a wife before my grandmother but she died. He had a son with his first wife but I never met him. Legend has it that my grandmother was not the nicest of stepmothers so the boy chose to live with *his* grandmother when the two got married.

My grandmother is the sixth of eight children. She was raised by her father, Samente because her mother died giving birth to her youngest sister. My grandmother says that she was chosen for my grandfather. His brothers saw her and thought she would be perfect for him after the death of his first wife. The two didn't even meet before getting married. My grandfather's family brought the cows for her bride price to her father and there it was, she was now a wife, a wife to a man she had never met. She says that she was his wife for a full week before she met him. He was away at work when his brothers took her and she had to wait for him at his family's house because they were married. She was already doing her wifely duties when they finally met. Legend has it that when my grandfather saw her, he complained about them getting her a short wife.

By a miracle that romanticized twenty-first-century relationships will never know, these two made that whole situation work. Their marriage worked; they had ten children together. Of the ten, two died at two months old and eight survived all the way through adulthood although only four are alive now. My grandparents raised their children with the same level of love and attention. Well, that's what my grandmother says but my aunts and uncles disagree. The youngest is now past his forties and still laments about not being the favorite child.

Eight children, born to and raised by the same parents, in the same town, with the same opportunities but such vastly different lives. Let's start with the eldest, Dido. Dido was the rebellious child. He found pleasure in breaking every single rule. My grandmother said he would wake up in the morning, get ready for school, put on his school uniform but never make it to the school grounds. Instead, he would meet up with his other rebellious friends and share his lunch with them. Dido's rebellion carried through to adulthood; what once was a problematic child grew into a problematic adult. As a priest of an orthodox church, my grandfather had strict no smoking, alcohol drinking and pork eating rules in his house. When I was eight years old, Dido had his own house but would visit his parents almost every day. I remember him talking to my grandfather in the garden. When my grandfather smelled the alcohol on his breath, he grabbed him by his temples, pressed his uncut nails through his skin and only stopped when he saw blood dripping down his fingers. Dido was on his knees, in front of his father, begging for forgiveness. Dido spent most of his life in and out of hospital. If he wasn't beaten to a pulp during a bar fight, his liver was giving him problems. Dido died in 2010 after a long battle with alcoholism.

The second born is Sno, the most beautiful of all the girls. Golden skin with hair that denies her Xhosa roots, flows like that of a mixed child. It is this hair that coined her the nickname "Nomakula " which means "Indian woman" in Xhosa. When she was eighteen years old, Sno fell in love with a much older man and has been with him since. It would have been cute if she hadn't changed the entire course of her life to follow this man from city to city depending on which post office he was commissioned to work at. You can still feel the rage in my grandmother's voice when she tells the story of how she had to go find her in Durban. My grandmother still hurts as a result of her actions because she wanted her daughter to be educated.

"Ndandimfundisa, akafuna!" (I was educating her and she refused it): my grandmother says every time they have an argument.

Sno and the postman got married and moved back to Cala when she got pregnant with their first child. He quit his job at the post office when they moved back, and has never been able to find another permanent job. Sno has been the breadwinner in her family for as long as I can remember. She worked at the biggest grocery store in town as a cashier for over twenty-one years! Say what you will about her, but this woman can commit. The store was bought by a major supermarket and Sno was one of the older employees who lost their jobs. They were told the store needed younger people who have basic knowledge of how computers work. Sno now lives in Cala, unemployed and surviving on a pension from the government.

Then there is Phumzile, his name literally means to "give rest". My grandparents had high hopes for this one and in part, he delivered. Phumzile is what ambition without action looks like. He carries himself with a pride that men of great stature have mastered. He once was the best boxer in town, one of the first Black bus drivers in our province and a man who I know to seamlessly carry anxiety and rage all at once. Phumzile is that brother that they all fear and also, all fear for. His punch can send you flying to the ground and his anxiety attacks leave *him* crippled on the ground. He stopped going to school in grade 5 but he has taught himself everything he needs to know, including English. Instead of paying for his own education, Phumzile married a woman who had great potential to be a teacher and he made it his goal to make sure that she got educated. Like most of these partnerships, she drives the nice cars and he lives in her shadow and numbs his pain by being promiscuous. Phumzile lives in Cala, in a marriage that should have ended decades ago and makes babies with women who are drawn to his wallet.

Vuyeka, only a year younger than Phumzile, was the sister who was actually my mother. I grew up idolizing this woman; there was no cooler human being in my eyes. She lived most of my younger years in Johannesburg and would come to visit us every Christmas. She would show up with bags full of Christmas clothes and hugs that lasted 'till I fell asleep on her chest. Vuyeka was an absolute joy. The house was loud and joyous when she came home. She would spring-clean the house every time she came home. Blankets and carpets would be lined outside as she would clean every corner of our small house. Vuyeka married a man who didn't deserve her, not even as an acquaintance. I think she didn't know her worth, that's the only way to describe the type of love she gave him. Her abusive husband couldn't stop her from wanting to be better! That's why, at the late age of 27 years, she enrolled herself in high school. She was determined to have a high school diploma and endured the embarrassment of being far older than her classmates like the queen that she was. She lived in Queenstown where she worked for a non-governmental organization hired to improve public school infrastructures in our province. Vuyeka died of HIV/AIDS-related pneumonia in 2002.

Nonci is the fifth child. He was born on the 28th of April 1968. I know this because my grandmother can't understand how the only child who was born on her exact birthday (28th April) is the most different from her. My grandmother is strong, independent and does her damnedest to ask nothing of no one. Nonci on the other hand, well let's just say that he walked this earth as if he was owed help. He demanded it from his brothers and sisters but *expected* it from his mother. When Nonci got married, he expected his wife to treat him like a king and her refusal to bow to a king with no throne ended that marriage with a quickness! Nonci, like all the other children, was strong-armed into going to school but nothing worked. He, for a few years, was a taxi driver, driving the long distance from Cala to Johannesburg. He thought it was so cool that he had a perm and wore tight pants like city folk. He was fired by the man he worked for because he came to work drunk a few times and we don't need to discuss drunk driving. Nonci died in 2016, suffering from HIV/AIDS-related illnesses and alcoholism.

The name "Mandla" is a boy's name and it means strength in isiXhosa (one of eleven official languages of South Africa). It is said that when my grandmother was pregnant with Nomandla, my grandfather was convinced that it was a boy. He then did something that he hadn't done before - he named her way before she was born. When a girl came out, he said well, she is Nomandla then. He believed that she was resilient and strong. Nomandla did and continues to do everything with the weight of her name. The first and only University graduate in her family, she lives life with a refusal to give up, a desired but sometimes dire attribute. She is the first to tell you that she stayed in an abusive marriage because she is "strong." She carries the burden of taking care of her ailing mother, raising her dead brother's four sons, all the while providing for her own two children. Nomandla is also the only one to ever live in Johannesburg where she is a teacher. She is the embodiment of a strong Black woman, the highs and lows of that narrative shine through her half-crooked smile.

Mzu was short, small in stature and walked like he was hoping to find a bag of money on the ground, his back slouched and arms tightly wrapped around it. He didn't really smile but when he did, you'd wonder why he didn't do it often, his straight white teeth lined the inside of his mouth like a well-kept curtain. I was a bit older when Mzu quit high school. I remember my grandmother begging him to at least finish grade 12 but when his grade 10 report card came and he had to repeat the grade for a third time, he simply said "no." He threw himself into doing menial jobs with the hopes of saving enough money to start his own farm. He was the most like his father in that sense, livestock and a blooming garden were the ultimate goal. Mzu had two failed marriages; he was abusive to his wives and they would leave him - a decision that made my grandmother look down on them and pity him. My grandmother is from a time when a woman needed to persevere in marriage. Mzu died in 2018 shortly after his second wife, with whom he had four sons, left him for another man.

Anele is the last born, you know him from chapter one. The man whose talents were buried in the infertile soil of expectations. You also know that he still lives in Cala as one of the four remaining children that my grandmother birthed.

Then finally, there's yours truly...ME! I was raised by these two human beings in the same conditions that they raised these eight human beings. Here's the story: My mother (Vuyeka) was eighteen when she was pregnant with me. She found out that she was pregnant and her first brilliant idea was to run away from home. She was scared shitless of her parents but mostly her mother. Vuyeka took cover at a convent in a nearby town, Ngcobo, where she was housed by the nuns. She and Nomandla were inseparable and that is why the first letter she wrote in "exile" was to Nomandla. Fearing for her sister's life, Nomandla gave the letter to her father who, without hesitation, made his way to Ngcobo, a town only an hour's taxi ride from Cala. He found Vuyeka and brought her home. After going through their options which included an abortion, my grandparents agreed to send my mother to my grandmother's brother's family in Whittlesea and that is in fact where I was born.

I am told that I was the joy of my grandfather's heart, his pride and the apple of his eye. He was, by all definitions of what a father is, mine. My grandfather saved the last piece of bread, he made sure that there was always milk for me when I got home, he washed me, cooked for me and when he had to, he disciplined me. When he died in 1994, I became my grandmother's responsibility and she did the very best that she could. She was a prison cook making R600 ($60) a month and was the sole provider for my family. Granted, we weren't such a big clan anymore, most of my aunts and uncles were married with children at this point but some still came to her for food and money. Did I tell you that she did the very best that she could? She really did. When I turned thirteen, I moved to Queenstown to live with my mother and that is where I finished high school. The man she married hated me but my mother begged me to endure because schools were so much better in Queenstown. I was in my last year of high school when she died. My grades left much to be desired and my father (who I met when I was thirteen) convinced my grandmother to let me move in with him and his family in Johannesburg. I was to repeat the last year of school in order to improve my grades for University. I did. My stepmother hated me but I had a goal. One year and I would be in Cape Town studying to be a lawyer. I went to University and graduated with a BA in Psychology.

Just to sum up my long life, I feel like I have lived a thousand lifetimes. In 2010, I left South Africa to teach English in South Korea. I then left South Korea to teach English in Malaysia because I wanted to be closer to a girl who lived in Singapore. In 2013, I went to the University of Peace in Costa Rica where I obtained an MA in Gender and Peacebuilding. I have failed businesses in the Philippines, I taught English to Monks in Thailand. I lived in Australia, also followed a girl and now I live in the United States with that girl. Pew! I feel like I was spitballing that.

My grandparents raised nine completely different human beings. Believe me, when I say this, they did the very best that they could. They had the same set of rules, the same desire to see success in each of them. Growing up in the oppressive apartheid era, my grandparents knew that what would get their kids out of poverty was education. My grandmother worked for years as a prison cook and most of her minimal salary went to paying for school fees and food. My grandfather was a priest of a small church and had no salary. He contributed to the household with his monthly salary and by making sure that the garden was healthy and growing good vegetables and fruits. My uncles and aunts have the same childhood but different excuses.

My uncles and aunts (and mother) and I have the same reasons and facts. WE were all born in apartheid South Africa where Black children had no quality education. The apartheid government created two different education systems, one for Blacks and one for Whites. The Bantu education was the system that Black South Africans were taught in. It was the most basic of all learning as the powers that be believed that the black mind could not comprehend complex subjects such as physics and mathematics. Therefore, black schools were to only teach simple mathematics and basic english. They were preparing Black children to be teachers (within the same system), nurses (never doctors), and what every White family wanted, a Black woman who spoke English and Afrikaans to raise their children.

The apartheid laws were only abolished in 1994. By then my aunts and uncles were much older. So, when it comes to access to education, all eight had the exact same hand to play. I am the in-between product of during and post-apartheid South Africa. Things didn't get much better because apartheid ended but they certainly changed. I reaped the fruits of a more integrated South Africa in Queenstown. I attended a colored high school. Not as good as the private schools but much better than the schools in the villages. I had better resources and a good quality education.

All nine of us were raised in extreme poverty. They often share stories of their poverty-stricken childhood. Their clothes that my grandmother would get from the nuns at the convent where she used to work before cooking for prisoners, Nomandla's jeans that she would wear all seasons. She would carefully cut the knees to embrace summer fashion and sow them back together when the cold winter came. They all had nights where all they ate was dry bread and sugar water. I was alive during the bread and sugar water era. However, whenever I want to join in on the poverty conversation, they all agree that I didn't have it as bad as they did.

Same parents. Same town. Same opportunities. Same stories. But such different lives. Who is responsible then? Nature? Nurture? A strong will? Survival? God? The ancestors? When I look at each of our lives, I am convinced more than ever that it is the choices that we make that define the lives that we live. We are responsible. It is empowering to know that, isn't it? Because that knowledge should make you want to change if you are not okay with the life that you lead. The fact that this is all on you - yes, there are outside influences, but when it's all said and done when the last song has been sung and the lights turn off, it is all on you. There is no one to blame in this game of living. You are dealt the cards but the game plan, well you are responsible for that.

My family is a prime example of those cards. We could say otherwise if we had all turned out the same. If none of us had made something beautiful with our lives, then maybe just maybe, we would make a list of things to blame. But, the fact that we all had the same circumstances and yet produced different results shows you that we are responsible. *I call you to responsibility.* I call you to a deep understanding that a victim mindset will keep you in chains. What will liberate you is knowing that taking responsibility for your own life will set you free. Listen, I know, I know that it is easy to blame people, blame your childhood trauma, blame your upbringing, blame your parents, blame the bullies that took your lunch and made fun of your broken shoes, the list is endless but all that blame does absolutely nothing for you. Instead, it keeps you limited. Limited to what you can be and what you can achieve.

Let's get to work! Grab that pen.

～

1. What are some events in your life that made you feel disempowered?

_____
_____
_____
_____
_____
_____
_____
_____
_____
_____
_____
_____
_____
_____
_____
_____
_____
_____
_____
_____
_____
_____
_____
_____
_____
_____
_____
_____

2. Of these events, which ones can you take responsibility for?

_____

_____

_____

_____

_____

_____

_____

_____

_____

_____

_____

_____

_____

_____

_____

_____

_____

_____

_____

_____

_____

_____

_____

_____

_____

_____

_____

_____

_____

_____

_____

_____

_____

3. How do you feel after taking responsibility?

_____
_____
_____
_____
_____
_____
_____
_____
_____
_____
_____
_____
_____
_____
_____
_____
_____
_____
_____
_____
_____
_____
_____
_____
_____
_____
_____
_____
_____
_____
_____

I should confess, that the first time I did this, I broke down. I screamed and thought how cruel. I was a child. I was helpless. I had no options. But when it finally kicked in, my need to be free, I came up with how I was responsible for every single thing that has ever happened to me. I owned some shit and boy did that give me power. My abusers were no longer in control of how I felt about myself, I was. Here is what one of the points looked like.

"My stepfather kicked me out of the house" (victim). "It was my responsibility to tell my grandmother and ask for her help" (responsibility).

I know that this is going to be very hard for you because, like so many of us, people have done some very shitty shit to you. The goal of this is not to make you take away accountability from those who have hurt you, no, it is to take back your power. As you go down this list of heartache, betrayal, pain, and anguish, I want you to FEEL all of it. Cry if you must, step away from it if you need to but get back to it. Also notice, pay attention to how much strength this exercise gives you.

LIVE, RESPONSIBLY

Six

Live, Honestly

"Stop blaming God for your decisions"

— JOSEPH OKECHUKWU, DIRECTOR AND ACTOR

Indy's grandfather (Papa) prays before every meal - every single meal! He drags himself to his long table in his two-bedroom condominium in Tri-cities, WA, sits at the end of the table and quietly gestures for us to hold hands in prayer. We take turns praying and when it is his turn, he always says "God, please heal me from this pain." Wait, I skipped a whole lot of information here. Who is Indy and why are we talking about her grandfather? Indy was my partner for five years, and up until recently, my world revolved around her. She *is* my home; it is crazy how some things just don't change no matter how much you wish them to. For five years, home was not a location for me, home was wherever Indy was. Whether that was in a 300 sq foot apartment in the heart of the city in Seattle or squatting in the basement of a friend's house because we were low-key homeless, none of that mattered. I was home, wherever she was. She was my love and she still is all that I perceived as good in this world. I am writing this chapter in Mexico, Puerto Escondido and my home is in Sydney, Australia. Life ferociously fell on our relationship, cracked it open, cracked us open and now, well we are scrambling for the parts of it that remain intact, hoping that out of them, we can create something beautiful. From surviving a pandemic, homelessness, crippling debt, multiple moves around the world, we simply couldn't survive where our relationship was taking us. We would each have to sacrifice a big, authentic part of ourselves to be together, a sacrifice that we were both not willing to make.

We met in the Philippines, Indy and I. I used to live in El Nido, Palawan, the most beautiful island in the world - according to people who know a lot of beautiful islands in the world - and Conde Nast Traveler is one of them. I spent three years of my life on this island, I had established a home, I had dogs, and a community. I ran businesses there, a party boat, an eco-resort and I co-managed a coffee shop. When Indy and I met, I was leaving all of that behind to start over somewhere different, and Thailand was my place of choice. I was going through a breakup - remember that breakup I kept "tabling" in chapter 2? Well, when it finally ended, I packed seven years of my life in one suitcase and a backpack. I didn't know that was even possible - to fit all that time, memories, experience and now; heartache, in one suitcase and a backpack. I did though. I filled the suitcase with clothes, the backpack with gadgets and prayed for the memories to swiftly unpack from my mind. What they don't tell you about memories is that they cannot be unpacked, they also cannot be drowned in alcohol or buried under a new warm body. Believe me, I tried to do all of that, weekends of absolute debauchery in Bangkok, a rebound girl (not Indy) whose heart I ended up breaking (because hurt people hurt people) and taking on new "projects" to help think of anything but this pain.

When I met Indy, I had returned from Thailand to do a final closure of my life in El Nido. I had come to get the rest of what I left, figure out what to do with the businesses, talk to my sister and try to end things differently with my ex. I had no plan of meeting someone new, and I wasn't even interested in "hooking up" with people. On the night we met, I had decided to go to bed early but one of my best friends who was in town with a tour group would not have it. She convinced me to go to the hostel they were staying in, have a few drinks with them and see how I felt afterwards. That was the night I met Indy. She was wearing a beautiful yellow dress that exposed her muscular back and showed off her strong legs. The straps hung on her shoulders as the dress flowed, lining her perfect curvatures, and demanding that I pay attention to every movement. Her golden hair lay perfectly on her shoulders making a perfect V-shape down her spine. She dragged her feet while playing pinball, and I prayed that she was looking at me as much as I was looking at her. My eyes wouldn't leave her. I watched her shy excitement when she made a shot, how her fingers wrapped around the red party cup when it was her turn to drink whatever alcoholic beverage was in it. I watched her look around, as if she knew she was being watched but when she would turn to me, I would swiftly look away. I let everyone around me know that I was into her. I said, "There she is, there is my wife. I want her."

After what felt like an hour of mentally stalking Indy, one of her friends came over to introduce themselves and she tagged along. The next thing I knew, my hand was fitted in hers as if it belonged. It is this that I miss the most, even in this separation, the way our hands would perfectly land on each other, how our fingers would interlock, how even in the silence, our hands would say "I love you." I looked into those big green eyes and I couldn't believe that a girl that beautiful was here, placing her soft hand on mine, looking at me in my eye. I recall resisting the urge to grab my heart and ask it to slow down. I only stopped staring at them when one of my friends came and rudely distracted me from trying to hear what those eyes were trying to tell me. After that "hello" my friend organized a game that would have us sitting next to each other and kissing in less than ten minutes. We played, whispered and held hands as we walked to the town's most popping club, Tikki Bar. We talked and we danced, and we ate and we danced some more. I needed to know her, but mostly, I needed to know about her.

"Who do you date?" I asked because I wasn't going to be dating any more straight/bisexual women.

"I date people," she said while taking another bite of her chicken wrap.

Not quite the response I was hoping for but also, she wasn't straight as my sister had insinuated when I pointed out the girl in the yellow dress to her. My sister was there during the breakup, she saw my ex-girlfriend make out with the boat captain who worked for me, she was there when I saw a text from the captain to my ex and she was there when I finally tapped out. She was witness to my pain and because of that, she wanted to protect me. When I told her I was interested in Indy, she said "Yes, she is stunning, but she is also straight, obviously straight." I didn't care, I still liked her. When Indy said she dates "people", I thought well, I can be "people" for the next few days, or maybe even one night. But fate or God had other plans. We kissed that night. After a slow slightly drunk walk back to the hostel where she stayed and where I had left my motorbike, I asked her to kiss me. Not quite the smoothest of moves, but I thought it was cute. "Can I get a kiss?" I asked as she started to walk away from me. She smiled, gave me the quickest kiss of my life and ran to the entrance of her hostel. I got on my motorbike, drove to my house with the biggest smile on my face. We had made plans to see each other the next day. I was going to drive her around the town and show her my favorite spots, the less touristy spots that we "locals" kept for ourselves but she told me she was sick and refused to see me. I convinced myself that she was blowing me off until my friend texted: "Hey, I just saw a yellow dress, she is really sick" My friends called her "yellow dress" for years after. That dress was truly a statement.

Turns out that she got sick from the ice! Crazy I know, but a lot of tourists got really sick from the ice in El Nido that year. We knew it was the ice because we had one ice supplier in the town. We all made sure our water was filtered so when people started getting sick, we tracked the bacteria to the ice supplier. I was so happy when my friend told me she saw her, not happy that she was sick, but happy that she wasn't ghosting me. I relaxed a bit, offered to bring her some remedies I knew but she said, "There is no way you will see me like this." We saw each other after two days, and what was regrettably her last night in El Nido. I took her to my favorite bar and ordered her my favorite drink - ginger mojito! It's divine. The thing about El Nido is that it is a tiny town. Everyone who came in knew me and would come over to say "hi." She was shy and beautiful. When we finished our first drink and I was getting ready to order the second one, she spoke.

"Okay, either we have a second drink or we go watch a movie at your place. We're not doing both."

We left.

We saw fireflies the first time we kissed. After those ginger mojitos, before going to "watch a movie," I drove us up to my favorite spot in town. It is a mountainside where during the day, you get the most beautiful views of the limestones that stick out of the ocean forming something out of the ordinary. This is what El Nido is famous for. The limestones have, over time, formed into gorgeous hills in the middle of the ocean, with stunning beaches. My favorite spot is where you stop to take it all in, to breathe in the beauty and the glamor of the island. But at night, you can't see shit. I used to come here at night to cry, but with Indy, I brought her to kiss her. We put our lips together, closed our eyes and I reached down with my arms around her waist. When the butterflies began to dance and our eyes slowly opened, we saw fireflies. It was magical. It's as if nature wanted us to be alone but surrounded, as if this moment, in the dark, had to be witnessed by someone or something.

At my house, where I really thought we'd watch a movie (I TRULY thought we would just watch a movie!), I set up my laptop and directed her to my bed. She lay, I lay next to her, and my heart lay between us, beating loudly and uncontrollably. I have been with women before but none ten years younger, Caucasian and with those deep green eyes. Ten minutes into the movie and our hands touched, fingers intertwined and lips locked. We took in what our bodies had to give, an exchange of pleasure and longing. I gave as much as I could and took as much as she would give. I thought "This is it, I am never going to see this girl again and I need her to remember me." I was wrong.

From that night, Indy and I followed each other to Indonesia, where we danced on a beach with a bottle of rum and coconut water. We made our way to Thailand where we taught English to Monks in our favorite town, Salaya and danced inside cages at clubs in Bangkok. We have lived in Australia where we drove through the outback and lived in Bondi Beach - the most beautiful beach in Australia. We have spent a month in South Africa where Indy learned that love is a language, spoken not with words but with gentle glances and across-the-room smiles. She and my grandmother were fluent in it. And now, it is 2023 and we have been living in America since 2020. We were also forced to pivot during the pandemic. We had plans, six months in the United States and we would be back on some island, dancing on a beach with a bottle of rum and coconuts in our hands. But...the pandemic. I'm sure you have said this as well: "I had plans...but the pandemic."

When we arrived in America, we lived with Papa for two months and this is how I know that he prays before every meal. His two-bedroom condominium where he lived by himself was a perfect setup for us to find our feet and figure out what we were going to do in the midst of this uncertain time. He also welcomed the company. COVID had isolated people and the fear of how long we were going to be alone was burdensome. Indy told me that Papa was a Pastor for many years and so I wasn't surprised by the number of Bible and hymn books on his coffee table. He was also an amazing singer, I had seen videos of him conducting the choir and the keyboard in the living was also not a surprise. Papa can sing! And Papa loves to sing. It is as if his compact, short and stocky body was built solely for those vocal chords. Papa also loves God. He speaks of God like he is speaking of a lover. I mean, I guess you have to in order to be a pastor but it's been a long time for me, hanging out with God-loving people like Papa.

Papa is also in a lot of pain: he takes an average of thirty pills a day! That's not an exaggeration, it's just that, thirty pills a day! I couldn't hide my shock when Indy showed me his pills. How could one person take so much medication?! However, you can see that Papa is in a lot of pain, his hands are constantly swollen, he spends most of his time in front of his TV and he grunts in agony each time he takes a step. He also drinks eight ounces of Asea water a day. If you don't know Asea, it's basically salt water that is supposed to have healing properties. It's also one of those multi-level marketing schemes and the founder has convinced many people that his salt water (think about that time you mistakenly swallowed the water in the ocean) can cure them of their ailments.

Papa once dared to suggest that it can cure HIV/AIDS, so we decided to agree to disagree on that one. This was after I had told him that my mother died of an HIV/AIDS-related illness. He exclaimed, "Man, I wish she could have gotten some Asea." There is nothing you can say to Papa that will make him stop drinking his Asea. He was once a distributor and still gets a box a month. Papa is also overweight and the doctors have repeatedly told him that weight loss would dramatically improve his health. So, with the sodium and the food, we are not sure if he is swollen, just overweight or both! When I showed concern for the amount of pain that he was in and wondered if there were other ways of managing it, Papa told me that he was okay with his pain because "God is glorified in it." I am a backslidden Christian and I am very well versed in the Christian language. So when Papa said this, I knew he meant that God wants him to be in pain because it would glorify Him. I had to say something and I reluctantly asked:

"How is a God that loves you glorified in you having a poor quality of life?"

"Because He knows you love him and can handle anything he gives you," he said defensively.

I watched Papa during our time together and I watched him when we visited him. He is the first person to tell you that "Khanyisa watches and observes" and I do. Indy and I did most of the grocery shopping and the one time he did a solo Costco trip, he came back with a box of chocolates, a bag of marshmallows, a box of cereal with loads of sugar and a gallon of fireball. We had him on our diet for the first few months and he allowed it. We cleaned out his kitchen cabinets of all the food that was high in sugar, filled the fridge with vegetables and convinced him to switch from soda to La Croix. He didn't go down swinging and that solo trip to Costco was his defiance. I couldn't believe that a man in that much pain was not willing to do anything that he could to heal. Yes, he prayed and I think he believed God was giving him that pain, but how could he not do what the doctors were telling him to do? Watching Papa's relationship with God and his health was a perfect example of the God Saga for me. The way in which we pass the responsibility of our lives to a higher power and release any form of accountability for our actions and our choices. There is something beautiful and yet disturbing about this kind of surrender. Faith gives us something we can believe, a hope that something and someone more powerful is looking out for us. But faith, coupled with sheer ignorance is dangerous and I dare say, disempowering.

I was also a tongue-speaking Christian like Papa and have used that

very same language to numb my pain and also honestly find someone
else to blame for my bad decisions. If it wasn't the devil trying to
sabotage me, it was God trying to teach me a lesson. I too believed that
every struggle and every trial was a sign of God's trust in my ability to
handle the big life stuff. I also said that God was glorified in my struggle
and when things were going well, I said it was God and not me who had
done the work. Yep, I was that person. I used God to soothe whatever
pain I was feeling, I used Him as an acceptable scapegoat for poorly
made decisions and I even used Him as a way to numb my grief.
Believing that God gave me the burdens made them a little easier to
carry. Here's a dissenting thought - what if it is all you? What if through
bad decisions and unhealthy habits, you have ended up where you are
right now? What if your problems are a manifestation of your inability
to control your life and your inhibitions?

Papa prays before he eats and his prayer goes something like this:

"God, thank you for this food, please take this pain away and heal
my body".

Papa has access to healthy foods, doctors who tell him exactly what
to do in order to live a healthier and longer life but yet, he doesn't do
any of that. He instead prays before every meal, and after that prayer, he
drinks a cup of his fireball whiskey and takes a handful of his mixed
nuts. It is not just him, we all do it. Changing our lives is very difficult,
and having something to blame for staying the same - well that's
convenient. We all have our own "saga." For some it is culture: I can't
tell you how many times I have heard people say "That's just my
culture." I have watched people accept unacceptable behavior and say it
is cultural. What is your saga? Is it your family? Do you allow them to
make decisions for you, tell you who and how you should be, control
every single move you make because "family is everything?" Whatever or
whomever you have given the responsibility of your life, the thing you
blame for where you are, your reason for pacifying your existence - that
is your God Saga.

Let's get to work! Grab that pen.

~

1. What is your saga? Is it God, is it culture, is it family?

_____
_____
_____
_____
_____
_____
_____
_____
_____
_____
_____
_____
_____
_____
_____
_____
_____
_____
_____
_____
_____
_____
_____
_____
_____
_____
_____
_____

2. Who is "glorified in your pain?" Who benefits from the life that you are living now?

_____
_____
_____
_____
_____
_____
_____
_____
_____
_____
_____
_____
_____
_____
_____
_____
_____
_____
_____
_____
_____
_____
_____
_____
_____
_____
_____
_____
_____
_____
_____
_____

3. What/who keeps you in your comfort zone?

Friend, when you start to own your life, fully, the good, bad, and the in-between - you are going to step into a level of power that you have never imagined. I want you to see a life that is not riddled with excuses and blaming of external things, but one that has learned to lean into its own phenomenal existence. I see you walk with the knowledge of the divine's support but not making that support the reason for being a passive participant in your life. I see you fully embracing that you are actually a co-creator with the Universe/God. I see you enter the arena of your life, actively participating, blow by blow and victory by victory. When you begin to see that all the divine power, that fire, lives in you! You are its flesh made manifest, what you desire, it desires for you.

LIVE, HONESTLY

SEVEN

LIVE, AUTHENTICALLY

"Authenticity is the daily practice of letting go of who we think we're supposed to be and embracing who we are."

— BRENÉ BROWN, AUTHOR OF *DARING GREATLY*

In Queenstown, the men's section at Edgar's, one of South Africa's biggest department stores, was directly behind the women's section, right next to kid's wear when I was in high school. The very first thing you would see walking in was the women's section and when my mother and I would go window shopping, I would walk right past it without even glancing at anything. I would excitedly take her to the men's section where I would show her my favorite pieces; jeans that would obviously fit loose on me with buttons instead of a zipper, the oversized shirts. But I knew not to take her to the men's shoes, even though I desperately wanted to try them on. My mother and I window-shopped a lot, so much so that I actually hate window shopping now. Window shopping to me is like that one thing you ate a lot as a child and now you just hate it. It doesn't make any sense to me; why would you put yourself through the torture of staring at things you know you can't afford? My mother was a serial window shopper. She and I would spend some Saturdays walking around town looking at all the major clothing stores and browsing at clothes she might want to buy in the future. When I saw something I liked, she would promise to buy it for me at the end of the month and when her paycheck arrived, it did not leave room for clothing shopping.

Not having enough money did not discourage her at all. She would excitedly try on her desired outfits and plan to buy them…at the end of the month. If we were not window shopping, she was planning her outfits for all the major events in my life. For my University graduation, she was going to wear a three-piece off-white suit with a big hat and white high heels. And then, at my wedding, she would wear a three-piece yellow suit, with a yellow hat and black heels. Her imaginary outfits resembled the outfits of the women we used to watch on the Trinity Broadcasting Network (TBN). She and I spent many afternoons planning graduation outfits and wedding outfits.

Vuyeka (my sister who was also my mother) loved to imagine what her children would turn out to be, even when we showed no signs of what she was seeing. Like, you can imagine that your child will be a vet because they like animals. No, my mother thought my brother Owen would be an accountant regardless of how much he barely passed accounting in high school. She didn't ask us what we wanted to be. She told us what we were going to be and what would make her happy. Part of the window shopping was for her to imagine me in some girly clothes. My mother would reluctantly follow me all around the men's section and then finally direct me back to the women's clothes where she would show me all the "cute" outfits. She would contend that those are boy clothes and perhaps I should look at the women's section. I have to tell you though, when my mother had the money to buy me a pair of jeans, she never forced me to buy a pair I didn't want. She would let me grab those oversized men's jeans and negotiate that perhaps I would get a more feminine top to wear with them.

My love of oversized boyish clothes started when I was a teenager. I didn't really care much when I was in primary school. I wore whatever my cousin Asanda, who was the girliest of girls, would pass down to me. Asanda loved all things pink and sparkly. The saving grace with her clothes was that because she was bigger than me, although girly, they would be baggy - providing the room my body craved. When buying me Christmas clothes, my aunts would always buy me a dress. A cute little girl dress that I would only wear on Christmas day and to church. The truth is that I don't know why my body needed to hide like that. It could have been the perpetual molestation from my uncles or the fear of men in general. I believed that looking like a boy would make me disappear, kinda go unnoticed. This grew with me and became part of my identity. Even when I wanted to be one of those girls who wore cute little outfits, somehow, my body felt more at home when I wore baggy jeans and oversized t-shirts.

In my high school, girls were allowed to wear long, gray pants (just like the boys) during winter and that was my favorite time of the year. I loved it - my white shirt tucked in those perfectly ironed gray pants that fell neatly on my shiny black shoes which I topped off with a green and white striped tie and a green blazer. Winter uniform made me feel like **me**. I felt comfortable and confident - and I loved the pockets. The winter uniform had a strict three month rule. Girls could only wear gray pants from June to the beginning of September. This was the only rule I broke because I was a good Christian girl. Every year, I would be sent to the principal's office for wearing my gray pants well past their allowed date - every year! He would reprimand me and ensure that I would be sent home if I was not in my proper uniform the next day. I would soberly dig for my green skirt, iron it for the next day to avoid being sent home. Just to be clear, I loved shorts, and I still do; it was the skirts and the dresses that didn't tickle my fancy. They required a level of femininity that I couldn't possibly reach.

Being in skirts and dresses felt like a restriction to me. I remember being pleasantly surprised when I realized that I could wear pants to my mother's church. It wasn't allowed at my grandfather's more orthodox church with very strict apparel rules. I assumed that all churches had the same rules. Turns out, they didn't! Most women at my mother's church would wear jeans and suits. They believed that God didn't care what you looked like on the outside, he was more concerned about your inside. Even my mom had a few blue jeans in her wardrobe that she would sometimes dress up for church. Although this was the case, I did not want feminine-fitting jeans, no, I wanted saggy jeans that folded all the way down my legs. Thus, my mother's discomfort. Although my mother tried to hide the discomfort, I could feel it. It must have been difficult to have one daughter and three sons and your daughter wants to be like the boys. I do know for a fact though, it is heartbreaking and lonely to know that the way you want to express your personhood causes discomfort to those you love.

After my mother's passing in 2002, I moved to Johannesburg to repeat my last year of high school. I moved in with my father, stepmother and two sisters. My school was for older children who had to repeat the last year of high school, and it was a Catholic school. We were all forced to adhere to Catholic beliefs and partake in every ritual. Did I say ritual? Yes, like Ash Wednesday is a ritual. Why are Christians not okay with calling their events rituals? I digress, my school was very intimidating for a village girl. The girls were stylish and pretty. Some wore very short dresses and others made sure their dresses showed off the top of their breasts. I felt like such an outsider in my baggy jeans and oversized t-shirts. After two months of attending school, my father gave me a thousand rands and told me to go shopping. I was ecstatic. I didn't want to be the Xhosa girl who looked like a boy anymore. I wanted to be a Johannesburg girl, stylish and sexy. Going against all my teenage rebellion, I went to the mall and bought a few skirts and a few tight-fitting tops. Not my regular regalia but I was determined to adjust and yes, to fit in. I made friends with two of the girls in my class and they showed me how to be a Jozi chick. I was a fast learner. By the end of that year, you would swear I was born in the city. Although my outside appearance graduated from the boyish clothes, my inside never got comfortable with looking like that. I felt like I had abandoned my favorite thing about myself.

I graduated high school with grades more than "just good enough" for University. I thrived and this time, I knew for sure that I was going to University. In 2004, I made my way to the University of the Western Cape, in Cape Town, another big city for this village girl. I was now accustomed to city life. Johannesburg, the biggest city in South Africa, had prepared me for whatever Cape Town was going to throw at me. I was also Jozi cool, which anyone will tell you is better than Cape Town cool. I slowly moved back to my tomboyish look and the independence of living without family made this return even that much easier. With no one watching what I was shopping for and having practiced looking like a lady-ish tomboy, I went back to the men's section of the clothing stores. I shopped for boy shorts and girlish t-shirts, and to balance out my look, I would top it off by wearing dangly earrings.

Things took a real turn in my last year of University. You see, although I was still a born again Christian and still very involved in the church, I started doing lesbian things with one of the girls in my Christian group. She and I became inseparable, and then we began getting intimate with each other. To have a successful disguise of our "friendship" I decided to dress super feminine again. My closet suddenly consisted of heels and tight dresses. I believed that dressing like this would hide that we were more than just friends. If we were both super feminine, there was no way that people would think we were physical with each other. That's what I thought anyway and I was wrong. People figured it out and they talked. Christians had the most to say. You can't hide attraction, you can't hide intimacy and definitely can't hide being in love with someone.

When I moved to South Korea, I was still a girly girl with short skirts and shiny purses. The made-up version of myself had successfully taken over the real version. That's what happens when we succumb to the pressure of being anything but who we are. We start to believe that the masks we wear are the true versions of ourselves. We believe that our made-up personalities and characters are the real us. We lose connection to who we truly are and live as who we are expected to be and who we pretend to be. We convince ourselves that who we created in order to fit in is the real us. This was me when I arrived in South Korea, completely immersed in the false versions of myself. The cis gender, heterosexual identity became who I was. It wasn't until that friend said "Hey Khanyisa, you know the best thing about living in a country where no one knows you. You can completely reinvent yourself, heck you can even choose a new name if you want to." Now, I have no desire to change my name, I love it. Khanyisa means light in Xhosa. My grandmother gave me that name believing that I would be the light of her life. However, the self-reinvention was titillating to me. I was intrigued and very curious about the ways in which I could redo my life.

It was that year that I decided to retire every single dress, skirt, purse, dangly earrings and any hyper-feminine thing I ever owned. I spent hours after school watching The L World, a TV show about a group of lesbians living and loving in Los Angeles. I then decided that I was in fact Shane, the "player" on the show. Shane wore men's clothes but made them look like they belonged on her woman's body. She walked with the swagger of an eighteen-year-old and her confidence made her sex appeal ooze. I wanted that confidence, that swagger, and that sex appeal. South Korea has the most amazing underground shopping centers and I had the money to spend. I was in control of what I wore because I bought it with my own money. I remember the first time I wore a bowtie. I felt powerful but most of all, I felt like myself. I shopped in the men's section and found clothes that suited my body and my personality. What I realize now is that I didn't reinvent myself in South Korea, rather, I *returned* to myself.

I tell you this tale of my wardrobe to remind you to fight for yourself, never grow weary of fighting for yourself. I want to call you to complete rebellion when it comes to showing up as you. I want to ask you to refuse an invitation that is attached to your denial of self. I beg you to refuse to sit at any table that needs to be comforted by you losing your authenticity. I also want you to know that what I am asking you comes at a cost, but that cost is worth it. The cost can be friendship; those who benefited from your self-abandoning might distance themselves from you. Your family might find your audacity to be different and repulsive. This world teaches us to hide parts of ourselves in order to fit in and to belong. But consider this, if you are not being yourself, you never stand a chance of experiencing true belonging. If you are not authentic, you don't fit in anyhow. True belonging can only be felt when we are being true to ourselves.

When I returned to South Africa after my stint in South Korea, my family had a difficult time reconciling with what I was wearing. The way I expressed myself was foreign to them, I was foreign to them. They could tell that I was not the person who left a year ago. I was new to them and they needed to decide if my newness belonged at their table. I remember one Sunday morning when my aunt invited me to go to church with her. I clothed myself in men's black dress pants, a long black shirt and red suede shoes, the type of dress shoe you'd only see on a man's foot. After church, one of the young girls came to me and said "Sis'Khanyi, I love your outfit, I particularly love your shoes, they look really good on you." I smiled and said, "Thank you." I have never forgotten about this compliment because it came at a time when I was fighting. I knew that there would be judgments, but I was done not choosing myself.

Were there negative comments? Absolutely yes! But here's the thing, the negative comments didn't sway me this time. They didn't make me feel bad about myself because I loved myself just the way I was. I felt beautiful. I did not need anyone to tell me if I was beautiful or not, I KNEW I was. This is the beginning of true freedom in my book when loving ourselves is not dependent on how others feel about us. Accepting ourselves doesn't depend on others accepting us. When understanding ourselves doesn't wait for us to be understood. This is the beginning of true freedom, this is the beginning of truly showing up as yourself when you decide exactly who you are and be unapologetic in showing up as that person.

It's your turn, babe. Pull out the journal and answer the following:

~

1. What made you truly happy when you were younger?

_____
_____
_____
_____
_____
_____
_____
_____
_____
_____
_____
_____
_____
_____
_____
_____
_____
_____
_____
_____
_____
_____
_____
_____
_____
_____
_____
_____
_____
_____
_____

2. What did you have to change about yourself to fit in?

_____

_____

_____

_____

_____

_____

_____

_____

_____

_____

_____

_____

_____

_____

_____

_____

_____

_____

_____

_____

_____

_____

_____

_____

_____

_____

_____

_____

_____

_____

_____

_____

3. If those closest to you really knew you, what would they know?

_____
_____
_____
_____
_____
_____
_____
_____
_____
_____
_____
_____
_____
_____
_____
_____
_____
_____
_____
_____
_____
_____
_____
_____
_____
_____
_____
_____
_____
_____
_____

4. How would it feel if you re-introduce yourself to them?

_____
_____
_____
_____
_____
_____
_____
_____
_____
_____
_____
_____
_____
_____
_____
_____
_____
_____
_____
_____
_____
_____
_____
_____
_____
_____
_____
_____
_____
_____
_____
_____
_____

I want to remind you that nothing has gone wrong with you. There is nothing about who you are that needs to be fixed or changed. You are exactly who you are here to be. Yes grow and if there is anything you want to lovingly change about yourself, then do. But who you are, the stuff that is true, and authentic about you is what makes you, you. Your difference is what makes you unique and the gifts you have for the world are wrapped up in that uniqueness. I know that this world has tried to convince you otherwise. You have been made to believe that who you are is inadequate and to belong, you have to try to fit in. You have been convinced that parts of you shouldn't exist in order for you to be accepted. I want you to know that true belonging and acceptance rely on your ability to show up as who you truly are.

Babe, let this be your permission slip to be unapologetically, fiercely and courageously..YOU! Let this be the moment you refuse to hide, or even conform. You are your most valuable, your most powerful when you let yourself be seen.

LIVE, AUTHENTICALLY

EIGHT
LIVE, DECISIVELY

"You cannot make progress without making a decision."

— JIM ROHN, AMERICAN ENTREPRENEUR AND
AUTHOR

I met my biological father when I was thirteen years old. As you know by now, my grandparents raised me as their ninth child, and the identity of my parents was a very poorly kept secret. As I told you in Chapter One, Cala is a small town and we know each other's secrets. However, when one of the ladies in the town called me "Vuyeka's child," I naively believed that that would automatically mean that her husband was my father. I relished the thought that Tsidi, Vuyeka's husband, is my father. He carried himself with a cleanliness that most of the men I had been surrounded by did not, his hair was always shaved on the sides and the top in perfect curls that just grew like that. His light skin perfectly matched mine, which made him being my father a great explanation for why I didn't have Vuyeka's darker complexion. Tsidi also claimed me as his own; he would make sure I knew the Christmas clothes were bought by him. He would call me "intombi yam" which means my daughter in Xhosa. I loved hearing him call me that especially after "knowing" that he is my father. So, I'm sure you can understand my confusion and dismay when Vuyeka sat me down at thirteen years old to tell me that someone else fathered me. Not only that, but he (the man who fathered me) wanted to meet me.

After a lot of resistance from my grandmother, because this man, Mzi, said I wasn't his child when my mother was pregnant, she finally agreed to allow the meeting to happen but under no circumstances would it be at her house. I met Mzi on a hot December Saturday afternoon, and I still remember his wide stretched arms when he approached and the smile that showed his perfect white teeth. I remember landing in between his arms, the innocence and safety I felt when he wrapped them around me. There was a strange familiarity about this man. He was not my father, not the way my grandfather was, but he was a man that even I, at thirteen years old, could see the physical resemblance I had to him. He made it clear to my mother that he was excited to get to know me and be my father.

One of Mzi's attempts to get to know me was a shopping trip to Queenstown, where he would buy me everything I needed and a few things that I wanted. He wasn't allowed in my grandmother's house so I met him at his family home just a ten-minute walk from my grandmother's house. His red BMW with tinted windows smelled like fresh leather, cologne and confidence. It was just the two of us. I excitedly placed myself in the passenger seat and he laughed when I told him that my grandmother said he was a gangster because of the tinted windows of his car. Now that I am thinking about it, as I am telling you this story, this was my first date. This man, not uncle or dad, not family nor foe, was someone who I knew I was supposed to love, someone who was making an effort to love me. We drove for about an hour and a half from Cala to Queenstown and our first stop was Wimpy's! One of South Africa's major fast food chains, think McDonalds meets an American diner. He pulled my chair out, just like I'd seen them do in the movies. A few minutes later, the waitress handed me the menu. I felt my stomach drop as I turned the pages with all the food options on them. Pages and pages of laminated food pictures, milkshakes, coffee and then desert which I had to choose from. I remember that menu as the first time I froze and felt anxious about making a decision! I felt very overwhelmed and Mzi ended up having to order for me because I could not decide what I wanted to eat.

This is what a lot of us experience in our lives, decision paralysis. We fear that we will make the wrong decision. We worry that what we choose will not get us where we want to go. Some of us worry that people will be disappointed by the decisions that we make. For me, it was all of the above - this difficulty in decision-making persisted throughout my life, whether it was choosing what subjects I wanted to do in school, right down to what I should choose to study as a career path. I seemed to always find myself stuck and waiting for someone to chime in and decide for me. It was my mother who decided that I should choose to study Law or Journalism. She argued that I had an inquisitive mind as well as the ability to argue, so those fields would suit my curious nature. My father (the new one) decided - through carelessness - that I should in fact not study law and I ended up studying Psychology. I was always afraid of making the wrong choice, or even worse, choosing something that would disappoint people. Making the wrong decision felt like an irreversible fallacy for me. It felt like something I couldn't take back, as if changing my mind would never be an option and that thought put more pressure on the need to make the right choice.

Many of us navigate life with a deep sense of angst and anxiety when it comes to making decisions. Whether we are aware of this nervous energy or not, we usually feel a certain type of debilitating anxiety when it comes to making life-changing decisions. Some of us become so paralyzed by this energy to the point where we remain prisoners of what we were deciding to change. Our response to the anxiety is choosing not choosing, which by itself, is also a choice. As adults, our lives are simply a collection of decisions, be it small or big, we are who we are, living where we live, and with whom we live with, because of the decisions made - by us or for us. I became a born again Christian, not because I understood what I was asked to believe, but because my mother decided that "she and her family will serve the Lord." I went to high school in Queenstown because my mother decided that it was a better school for me. I kept the abuse from my stepfather a secret because my mother decided that my grandmother didn't need to know.

The psychological term for the fear of decision-making is called decidophobia. It was coined by Walter Kauffman, a philosopher at Princeton and Harvard Universities. Decidophobia is a result of constant dependency on others to choose for you, as if we never outgrow having our parents make decisions for us. We just pass on the responsibility to other relationships in our lives. Extreme decidophobia manifests in different ways. It is in the anxiety you feel when you have to make a decision. It also manifests as procrastination: you fear making a decision so much that you end up procrastinating. There are also real and lasting consequences from decidophobia and a lot of us see it in the missed opportunities that we have experienced. Fearing to decide so much that we actually miss the good things that life has in store for us.

The antithesis to decidophobia is learning to cultivate self-trust and self-confidence in order to exercise our power to choose. As a coach, I am constantly asked about building self-confidence. People are keenly aware of their lack of confidence and the price they pay for that inner deficiency. Self-confidence is simply defined as the belief you have in yourself and your capabilities. Now, we have to recognize the role that trauma has played in some of us not having that self-confidence. It would be so easy if I just gave you a few exercises to build your confidence and send you on your way, but it is not that simple. Some of us have endured traumatic experiences whether big-T or even small-t traumas that impacted our ability to believe in ourselves. Either we grew up in environments where our caregivers paid a lot of attention to our inadequacies, pointing out every single one of our flaws and using them as justifications for punishment. Or, we were constantly reminded of the areas where we fell short, where we were not exceptional and no matter how much we tried to be excellent, it was never enough. I have a friend who told me a story about how his father would always have something negative to say no matter how much everyone else around him told him how good he was. A 98% score on a test was not enough, coming second during a race was similar to coming last, nothing he did was ever good enough. With each criticism, his father knocked his confidence and chipped aways at his worth. Without even being cognizant of this, my friend continued to live his life trying to live up to a version that was impossible to attain, the version that his father wanted him to live until he began to actively shift his narrative.

I want you to start paying attention to your own stories of confidence, self-esteem, and worth. This is very important for your journey of being a decisive and powerful human being. What experiences shaped the way that you believe about and in yourself? What narratives run around your mind when you have to make big, bold, life-changing decisions? Whose voices are so loud that they give you decision paralysis? What do the voices say? Who do they belong to and why do you believe them? For me, the voices belonged to so many of my guidance and authority figures but mostly my uncles. My uncles, all five of them were my first bullies, all five of them but to varying degrees. I was a shy, pretty subdued child, especially after my grandfather and that made me an easy target for them. Depending on how they were feeling, whether drunk or sober, happy or angry, I was their dumping ground for uncomfortable emotions. The physical abuse didn't stick as much as the verbal abuse did, and that is what ate away at my confidence. It was their sharp tongues that hurt more than their open hands and belts. It was their ill-intended "jokes" and mean-spirited comments that created the person who played small in her life. When I dug deep inside of me to find the source of my inability to believe in myself, it was their voices that would play in my head and heart. These are some of the things I would hear a lot about myself growing up.

"Khanyisa can't do anything right."

"Khanyisa doesn't listen."

"Khanyisa will fail in school."

"Khanyisa is always breaking things."

Nothing was ever good enough, and not only that, everything was a punishable mistake. A quick backhanded slap, a wet towel across my body, a switch that I would have to go pick out myself, or even a belt. When we are not allowed to fail, we are not allowed to learn. It is through learning that we discover our strengths, and sharpen our weaknesses. It is through learning and failing that we learn how to trust ourselves and how to believe in ourselves. When we are shamed for failing, we become afraid to try anything and that means we become afraid to choose.

What was my path to healing? I'm so glad you asked! It was looking at the people whose voices lived in my head and deciding if those voices were worth the attention I was giving them. I have given you a rundown of my uncles' lives in Chapter 5. What do you think, are those the examples of excellence that I should aspire to? I'm not saying that in a mean-spirited way at all but I had to learn that my bullies were insecure men who lived in a lot of fear and anger. I became aware of the fact that the stories I was repeating about myself were written by people who were incapable of writing amazing stories about their own lives and I decided that they were not the voices I should be listening to at all. I want you to do the same thing. Look at the lives of the people whose voices ring in your head, the people whose narrative you live in your life, who are they?! How are they? What have they done with their lives? So often, those messages are from their fears, their own reckoning with themselves and their projections. And what you are unconsciously doing is living out your life through other people's fears, failures and projections. Truly, dig into their life's path, without trying to judge them because that is their journey, but what you are doing is trying to decide if their voices are worth the space and control you have given them.

I also learned how to cultivate self-trust. There is a direct relationship between confidence and self-trust. You have to begin your confidence-building journey by building your trust in yourself. Start making yourself promises and coming up with non-negotiables. Start small though and only choose ONE thing. It can be as simple as drinking a glass of water in the morning or never missing a Monday at the gym. Whatever it is, choose it and keep that promise. The more you keep that promise to yourself, the more you start trusting yourself and the more you believe in yourself and then boom - there is your self-confidence. You are now becoming someone you can trust, someone you can believe. And that belief is going to trickle down into your decision-making. You will experience fear because it doesn't go away, but you will be courageous because now, you are someone that you believe in. You have proven yourself to be trustworthy.

The final, and perhaps the most crucial aspect of my journey, entailed relinquishing the victim mentality. The most emotionally grueling exercise I did when I was doing my Master's program in Costa Rica was during a self-development class. The professor asked us to write down every bad thing that had happened to us, even the things we felt like we had no control over. She then asked us to think about how we took part in our misfortune in those events. I wept. Like seriously cried because how dare she! How dare she suggest that I could have protected my young self from all the atrocious things that happened to me. I thought about all the abuse I had gone through and the pain I had experienced, things that shaped me from a young age and I could not help but think of her as a cruel person for even suggesting that I was in a way able to stop that. After the resistance, I sat with my teary eyes and really thought about how I could take any responsibility for it. To my surprise, I did. I owned my stuff and in that, I gained a power I never thought possible.

When you can own as much as you can of your story, you also permit yourself to change that story. When you can take credit for the choices you've made, even the shitty ones, you give yourself the power to make different choices. When I named the voices that were limiting me, I had to think about how I could silence them and not being their victim was a big part of that silencing process. To own my life in a way that felt both good and challenging, I had to start by owning my decisions and my choices. I had to own the choices I made, as much as the ones I did not make. This process is very difficult for those of us who endured difficult shit that we had absolutely no control over. However, owning the decisions that I made, and how they have impacted my life has been a really freeing journey. It is realizing that there is a point in our lives where the blame game doesn't work anymore.

Let's get you to reflect, you know what to do here.

~

1. What is your decision-making process?

_____

_____

_____

_____

_____

_____

_____

_____

_____

_____

_____

_____

_____

_____

_____

_____

_____

_____

_____

_____

_____

_____

_____

_____

_____

_____

_____

_____

2. Who do you usually consult when you have to make a decision and why?

_____

_____

_____

_____

_____

_____

_____

_____

_____

_____

_____

_____

_____

_____

_____

_____

_____

_____

_____

_____

_____

_____

_____

_____

_____

_____

_____

_____

3. What is the biggest decision you have made recently?

_____
_____
_____
_____
_____
_____
_____
_____
_____
_____
_____
_____
_____
_____
_____
_____
_____
_____
_____
_____
_____
_____
_____
_____
_____
_____
_____
_____
_____
_____
_____
_____
_____

4. What decision are you afraid to make in your life and why?

_____

_____

_____

_____

_____

_____

_____

_____

_____

_____

_____

_____

_____

_____

_____

_____

_____

_____

_____

_____

_____

_____

_____

_____

_____

_____

_____

_____

_____

_____

_____

5. What would your life look like if you made the decision?

_____
_____
_____
_____
_____
_____
_____
_____
_____
_____
_____
_____
_____
_____
_____
_____
_____
_____
_____
_____
_____
_____
_____
_____
_____
_____
_____
_____
_____
_____
_____
_____
_____

Let's imagine this life of confident and empowered decisions that you are about to embark on. I see you finally becoming the person who is not afraid of making decisions, someone who pushes past that fear, knowing that should they need to, they can change their mind. I see you having fully overcome your decision paralysis and being confident in the fact that you are the authority in your life. Not only this, I see life presenting you with so many opportunities and things to choose from because you are now a confident person who doesn't run away from opportunities because you are afraid to choose. I see this badassery for you! You are someone who asks for advice and seeks counsel but ultimately, you know that the final word belongs to you.

This level of empowerment has also let those you love in on the person you are becoming. They now know that your life is not a community project. The boundaries you have set with them in terms of who you are and how you want to conduct yourself are very clear. They know that you are someone who is not going to conform but you are someone who will weigh their options and confidently choose what is aligned with their values. Because you have built this self-trust, you also know what misalignment feels like and being deterred on your part through hasty decisions is not the case for you anymore. Look at you! This my darling is what it means to be the author of your life, and the captain of your ship.

LIVE, DECISIVELY

NINE

LIVE, PURPOSEFULLY

"The path to our destination is not always a straight one. We go down the wrong road, we get lost, we turn back. Maybe it doesn't matter which road we embark on. Maybe what matters is that we embark."

— BARBARA HALL, AUTHOR, EMMY-NOMINATED
WRITER AND PRODUCER

Why the fuck are you here!? What is the reason for your very existence? Purpose is defined as "the reason for which something is done or created or for which something exists." If we agree that we are created by something divine and outside of our human capacity to fathom, then surely there is a reason for that divine thing to create us. Peww. Did you let that land? Read it again. I was born to two teenagers who were not even dating when they conceived me! The story I know is that they each had a boyfriend/girlfriend and when my dad was visiting home (Cala) from a work break at the mines in Johannesburg, he and my mom had a little lust-making session at the back of the church and boom, there I was conceived. I am told of the fear, horror and sheer shame my mother felt when she found out she was pregnant. She was so afraid to tell her parents that she opted to run away from home and live in a convent in a neighboring town. When my aunt finally ratted her out to my grandparents, my grandfather went to pick her up and took her home where she faced my grandmother's fury. After multiple considerations of what she should do, one of them including an abortion that was suggested by a family friend, they all agreed to send her to live with my grandmother's brother's family in another province until she gave birth. The family's embarrassment was so deep that they couldn't have her walk around the town with a pregnant belly at eighteen years old.

In our community, in society, in my mother's family, I was the mistake that she made, a mistake that would forever change the trajectory of her life. I had an uncle who would call me "umgqakhwe" when he was drunk and that means "a bastard child." The phrase was a constant reminder to me of the mistake I made when I came into this world. At only eighteen years old when she conceived me, my mother had made a mistake that she would never recover from. She was now a mother. When I was a teenager, my mother actually took me to an OBGYN and tried to convince him to trick me into giving me birth control without my knowledge. He refused of course. The mistake my mother made was significant enough to drive her determination to prevent me from repeating it in any possible way. When I asked her why this was so important to her, she said "I worry that this mistake is hereditary. I am scared that it is something I can pass on to you." This was the first time my mother ever called me a mistake to my face. She would always say "You were unplanned, but you are not a mistake." When she was faced with the reality of my arrival and the fear of having me repeat her mistakes, she admitted that I was a mistake. I do not know who/what you believe in, but I have to tell you, there is something bigger, something that sees a mistake as an opportunity. Something that I knew from the very beginning, perhaps evident to the teenagers who brought me into existence, is that they perceived me as a mistake. However, to the divine entity, I was an intricately calculated, meticulously planned, and impeccably timed chance. I possessed a distinct purpose, and it is that purpose which currently has you engrossed in reading this book.

In our shared humanity and all the things that connect us no matter how much we want to highlight our differences, we all have the intrinsic need to know WHY THE FUCK WE ARE HERE. What is the thing that we are here to do and how do we find out? Purpose. Usefulness. The reason for our being. The very reason for our existence. The thing that was entrusted to us prior to our arrival. Some of us spend most of our lives trying to figure out what it is exactly that we are here to contribute, while others just live their lives moment to moment, not truly taking the time to figure it out. I wish that I could say that those of us who do not take on the challenge of finding out what our purpose it is because we want to live in the present, but that is simply not true. Some of us are in situations that call us to live in constant survival mode. We simply do not have the luxury of exploring the big thing we are here for. We simply need to know what it is that we are going to eat tomorrow, how we are going to have the money to educate our children and how we are going to take care of our elderly.

Some live life under the breathtaking weight of fear, constantly afraid of doing anything that will cause us to leave our comfort zone. We are so used to what is familiar to us even when we know it is no longer serving us or who we want to become. We would rather stay in that place of fear and discomfort than take the time to do the work of searching for what it is that life is calling us to be and do. The thing with purpose is that it WILL make you leave your comfort zone. You cannot be in pursuit of your higher calling and be grounded in what feels familiar and comfortable. And then there are those of us who agonize over what our purpose is, and I must tell you, I belong to this group of humans. It may be the fact that I grew up knowing I was a mistake, and I had to shift that narrative for myself. It is like when I find my purpose, which I have, I can go to all those people who told me and my mom that I was a mistake, and go IN YOUR FACE! Look, I was never a mistake, I had a purpose.

I told you that I was a born-again Christian throughout my teenage years and early adulthood, right? Well, A Purpose Driven Life by Rick Warren was one of the most popular books in Christian(dom) at that time and without having read the book myself, I knew that I had to live a "purpose-driven life." I can't tell you the number of sermons that I sat through and the minister would passionately preach about purpose and use this book as a reference. The men preaching about purpose felt like they had already figured out what theirs was...the preaching and telling us to find our purpose. These ministers looked and felt like they were sure of what they had to offer the world, and how lucky they were to have found it, and to have lived it. They also made finding your purpose sound like the finale of the things you had to accomplish, like that missing piece of the puzzle that would make the entire picture whole. It was a quest that we all had to embark on, but that quest shouldn't be about us, but the will of God. So, not only were we to find what our purpose was, but we also had to make sure that it was the will of God for our lives. And, that purpose had to be one thing! The thing.

I can still see that overly serious teenage girl, with a journal and highlighter at every church service, listening to the preaching and painfully needing to know - what is my purpose? At seventeen years old, SEVENTEEN, I was trying to answer the big question of my existence. I had to get it right! There is nothing I feared more than not being in the will of God and nothing I had to know more than what my purpose is. With all the sermons on purpose, being taught that we SHOULD have one, I don't remember being taught HOW to find it. What I understood about purpose at that point was that it had to be something bigger than me, that it had to be something that had nothing to do with me, but it most certainly had to be done by me. When I left the church, I couldn't shake off the deeply ingrained need to find my purpose. Not so much in the sense of having it be tied to God's will in my life but I had to find deep meaning in everything that I did. For example, when I went to teach English in South Korea, that job had to be more than just "teaching", it had to have a higher cause. Or, when I had my businesses in the Philippines, the money I made wasn't worth anything if I didn't attach it to something bigger, so I used some of it to send Filipino girls to University. There has never been a job where I didn't try to find a way to serve beyond the scope of the job description.

But through these years of searching and trying to understand my purpose, this is what I have come to understand:

1. We all have one.
2. We can all live in it.

What we do that is not of service to us or align with our purpose is to try to make it an abstract thing. It's like we wait for a voice from the heavens to come in those moments when we are half asleep and whisper to us what it is that we are here to do. We look for a purpose outside of ourselves, something we have to get bestowed upon us but the true purpose is internal. The true purpose is found in those quiet moments, the moments where you reconnect with yourself, see yourself and love yourself. Why these moments? Well, these are the times when you can actually turn off the noise of expectation. There is no one but you at these times. You with YOU! When you approach yourself with grace, compassion and curiosity, you begin to tap into what lies within. You get connected with your inner knowing, that which has always been but, through life's chaos, you've ignored. This is the time when you get connected to yourself and within that connection, you explore your innermost wants and desires. When you have completely learned to strip yourself of what you have been conditioned to want, the things you were TOLD should matter and unapologetically explore your truest needs, this is what will reveal your purpose. If purpose thend is wrapped up in our authenticity, to find it means we have to start embracing our truest selves. If purpose is the thing that YOU are here to do, then living as YOU is the first step to discovering it.

When I let go of the pressure to find my purpose and allowed myself to be authentically me, I discovered what it is that I am meant to do and who I am here to serve. I started by looking back to things that truly brought me joy when I was younger, the ways I loved to play, the things I was interested in, and there it was, my purpose. I was that teenager who used to run home after school to watch Ricki Lake, Oprah, or Noleen Maholwana Sangqu. When my schoolmates were deciding on the extracurricular activity they were going to partake in throughout the week, I was glued to the TV watching these women talk, connect and yes, coach. I traced it even to when I was younger. I was that random child who preferred to sit at my grandmother's feet with her friends and be enthralled by their stories. There was always something so appealing to me about the human experience, and these grown folk conversations brought me into that. I don't know what it is for you, but what do you find when you trace back to those years right before you were untouched by life and its seriousness? What are the things that you were curious about, the stuff that made you want to know more and pay undivided attention to? Let's try to find what you are here for in those moments of joy. Can we do that?

What about those tough life lessons? What if our purpose is neatly packaged within our pain? One of the reasons I became a Life Coach was pain. I sat in my studio apartment during the height of the pandemic and thought about my life. I think a lot of us did. It was during this intense, quiet facing of myself that I came face-to-face with my pain. All the stuff I had buried with being busy, moving from one country to the next, that it felt like the Universe was forcing me to sit with myself. I vividly remember saying: there has to be a point to all this pain, I couldn't have just gone through this for nothing. That is how getting certified as a Life Coach became something I had to do. I really believed that there was a purpose to my pain. I explored some dark parts of my life, from my mother's young death, her toxic relationship with my stepfather, the abuse I endured, my church trauma - I allowed myself the grace and compassion to look at it all. When I did, I knew that I had to use it to help others. I had to use these stories of pain and darkness and turn them into light for someone else. I work with women who feel stuck in their lives, women who do not know what is next for them and, through my story of pain and triumph, I am able to guide them. What if you did the same? Look at your pain instead of avoiding it. You don't have to become a life coach or even write a book, but what can you do with what life has used pain to teach you?

What I have come to understand about purpose is that however you perceive it, whether big or small, for it to be purposeful, it must be in service of others, and it must be in service of you. First of all, I want you to know that there is nothing wrong with feeling good when you are in service. My very first venture was a non-profit foundation called Agape Love Foundation. I ran this non-profit with my ex-partner and we did some amazing things for others and doing those things made us feel good in the process. Our very first project was renovating a kindergarten in the Philippines. We were on vacation and one morning, on our way to get what we decided were the best pancakes in town, we saw a group of small kids in cute blue and white uniforms entering a building that looked like a deserted warehouse. On our way back from breakfast, we saw these little people playing outside the school and we decided to go in and say "hi." The teacher came to greet us at the door with a huge smile and we asked about the school. She walked us around the property, beachfront land and then told us about what the kids needed. Their priority was a new floor, a stronger bamboo wall and windows. We then spent the rest of our two weeks in El Nido renovating a kindergarten and making friends with the community. I can't tell you how good it felt for ME to watch little people be so excited over a new floor and windows. Man, the things we take for granted in life! This project was for the community: we served, we created and it felt good for us too. We jumped out of bed with so much excitement those weeks because we were doing something that mattered to others, we were in service. So, when you decide what it is that you want to do with your precious life, I hope you find as much joy in it as the ones you serve with it.

Let's get into your purpose.

~

1. What do you feel about your life? Are you living for your purpose?

_____
_____
_____
_____
_____
_____
_____
_____
_____
_____
_____
_____
_____
_____
_____
_____
_____
_____
_____
_____
_____
_____
_____
_____
_____
_____
_____
_____
_____
_____

2. If yes, what is that purpose and if no, what is missing for you in what you are doing right now?

_____

_____

_____

_____

_____

_____

_____

_____

_____

_____

_____

_____

_____

_____

_____

_____

_____

_____

_____

_____

_____

_____

_____

_____

_____

_____

_____

_____

3. I want you to reflect on your childhood, those moments of pure childhood joy. What would you be doing?

_____

_____

_____

_____

_____

_____

_____

_____

_____

_____

_____

_____

_____

_____

_____

_____

_____

_____

_____

_____

_____

_____

_____

_____

_____

_____

_____

_____

4. What can you do now as an adult to reconnect with that joy?

_____

_____

_____

_____

_____

_____

_____

_____

_____

_____

_____

_____

_____

_____

_____

_____

_____

_____

_____

_____

_____

_____

_____

_____

_____

_____

_____

_____

_____

_____

_____

_____

_____

5. From that joy, what can you create that feels like purpose for you?

_____

_____

_____

_____

_____

_____

_____

_____

_____

_____

_____

_____

_____

_____

_____

_____

_____

_____

_____

_____

_____

_____

_____

_____

_____

_____

_____

_____

_____

_____

_____

I read that 76% of the global workforce is excruciatingly unhappy and unfulfilled in their chosen careers. I also read that 54% of managers are unsatisfied with the work that they do and how they contribute to society. This means that over half of the global population is experiencing a sense of dissatisfaction, and for some that dissatisfaction manifests in toxic work environments that could lead to mental health issues. Research shows that there is a correlation between life's purpose and being a healthy person. People who believe that they have something to live for are more prone to taking better care of themselves. That is not just physical, but also mental, financial, and spiritual. When you find your purpose, you not only find something you are here for, but you also find something for which you will do everything to live.

I want to imagine this purposeful life with you, love. When you discover what it is that you are here to give, and perhaps to get, what will your life look like? I see you being more intentional with your life. I see you being more intentional with the way you navigate your relationships because you know, you have so much more to live for now. I see you being more joyful; you have a goal now, something that can only be done by you. Something that you know humanity will miss out on if you do not do it.

LIVE, PURPOSEFULLY

TEN
LIVE, SELFISHLY

"Finding yourself is actually returning to yourself. An unlearning, an excavation, a remembering of who you were before the world got its hands on you."

— EMILY MCDOWELL, WRITER AND ILLUSTRATOR

"I will not grow old with this person" is the last thing my mother said to me about her marriage - she died six months later. She had gotten into a terrible fight with her husband. He was drunk, as per usual, and this time, he was an angry drunk. My stepfather lived in only two states when he was drunk: he was either super loving or super angry. We could always tell which drunk he would be by the face he wore when he entered the house. He didn't need to speak, we all knew how to read him, then act accordingly. When happy, he would walk in with a smile plastered across his face, he would be careful about knocking things over as he would stumble towards my mother for some affection. When angry, he would quietly walk in, eyes bloodshot red and he would look at us like we were the thorn in his flesh. He would point out everything his drunk was telling him was wrong with the house, the food we'd cooked and for some of us, it was the sound of our breath that made him violent.

The day my mother said she wasn't going to grow old with him was an angry drunk day. He came home in the late afternoon, started yelling and screaming accusations of infidelity towards my mother, and his usual go to "I want Khanyisa out of my house." This time, she was tired of obliging and she fought back. My brothers and I sat silently in the living room, hoping that the sound of the TV would drown out their voices - it didn't. I was surprised when my mother came out of her bedroom untouched, physically but there was a resignation in her eyes that even I as a teenager couldn't miss. She asked the boys to stay with their father while she and I went for a drive. As she got in the car and began buckling her belt to drive, she turned to me and said "I will not grow old with this person." I can still remember my relief and thinking, finally, she is finally going to leave him. She was done, and I could feel it. She wasn't angry, she wasn't crying, she wasn't disappointed, she was simply tired.

That was the last fight I witnessed between my mother and stepfather because she got sick a few weeks after that. Her illness progressed at a speed that I didn't think was possible. She was in and out of the hospital for about four months, she rapidly lost weight, she stopped going to work, it all happened so fast. After a week and a half in hospital, she died from pneumonia. It wasn't until a year after her death that I found out that my born-again Christian mother died from an HIV/AIDS-induced illness. I was told that after doing multiple tests and not figuring out why her lungs kept failing, the doctors were able to convince her to get an HIV test and that came back positive. My mother stayed in a marriage that ultimately killed her. I was told that it wasn't so much the diagnosis that ended up taking her life more than it was her response to the diagnosis. South Africa was at the height of the HIV/AIDS pandemic, which means there was so much fear and stigma around those who had the disease. Not only that, my mother had lived her life as a woman of God. She wasn't promiscuous, or unfaithful, which are the labels that were given to those living with the disease. I was told that it was her stress, her inability to accept the diagnosis that killed her only two days after she was told of her HIV/AIDS status.

My mother was with her husband for over eighteen years. She had followed him to Johannesburg only three months after she gave birth to me, leaving me with her parents. She changed her life around, forsook all that she knew to be his partner. My mother bore three beautiful sons for him, she endured a slew of mistresses, physical abuse as well as verbal and emotional abuse. She took every single one of his family members in when they were having a difficult time as if she had enough to give. My mother LOVED that man. She loved him so much that it killed her! Now, you are wondering what this sad story of my mother's untimely death has to do with you and here it is.

In 2020, I was in a 300-square-foot studio apartment with Indy, and our dog Oliver. I was in America on a tourist visa and it was becoming clear that COVID was going to be more than just a few months' inconvenience and we were going to have to pivot, and make different life plans. My immigration status in America quickly turned from "tourist" to immigrant. I was also faced with the question of "What am I going to do now?" What was this time calling me to do and in that uncomfortable silence, isolation and self-introspection - I began to think about my mother's young life. I thought about her not so much as my mother, but a woman I knew and loved. I thought about how she showed up in this world, I thought about the toxic relationship she had with my stepfather and the reasons she gave for staying in that toxicity. I thought about her in moments when she wasn't his wife and she was just her. I thought about her joy, that loud laugh, and man, I thought about her hustle. How she once had three jobs! And when I sat with these bitter-sweet memories of my mother, I wondered, how someone that magnificent died so young. Thirty-six years is way too young.

Not only did I use the forced self-introspection of COVID to think of my mother, but I also thought about myself. I thought about what I had learned from her and how those lessons had consciously or unconsciously shown up in my own life. The biggest indicator of those lessons was that breakup I told you I kept tabling in the Philippines. One of the thoughts I had during that heartbreak was "I am acting like my mother" and it was this thought that helped me cultivate the courage to leave. I was the woman who was focused on the person my partner was cheating with instead of her behavior. The recurring theme in how my mother and I showed up in those relationships is self-abandonment. We lost our agency, our character and completely ignored our needs, safety and health in order to save a relationship, and in my mother's case, a marriage.

When we self-abandon, we lose the most important relationship in our lives - the relationship we have with ourselves. What many of us do not realize is that healthy relationships with others begin and end with healthy relationships with ourselves. We do not realize that because we are raised in a society that teaches us that it is selfish to put ourselves first. Think about it, how many times have you been called "selfish" when you said "no", when you expressed your desire to put yourself first. How many times have you been labeled as self-centered when you chose to take care of your own needs first, and you are made to feel guilty for choosing yourself. We are surrounded by people who benefit from our people-pleasing, self-sacrificing, over-compromising and self-abandonment. These are people we love and we want to do anything to keep them in our lives, but so often, keeping them comes at the cost of losing ourselves. We camouflage ourselves and shapeshift to whoever they expect/need us to be in fear of their rejection.

The return to self, the repair of this most important relationship requires a deep sense of self-introspection, giving yourself the gift of your own love, and yes, being selfish. This journey begins with self-awareness. The mistake we make is focusing on who we want to be and avoiding who we are right at this moment. I know it is fun to dream about who you want to become when you "arrive" but before you even journey, I want you to look at who you are right now. I know there are things you would rather not face, but this journey to yourself requires you to face them. That is the only way you are going to fix them. For me, I had to accept that I was a people-pleaser, that I was someone who self-abandons in relationships because of my abandonment wound and fear of being rejected. This acknowledgment wasn't easy, not by a long shot. However, it allowed me the courage to heal. When I stopped hiding, and when I stopped pretending to be someone I was not and faced the truth of who I actually was, I started to learn the things I needed to learn with more intention.

In that process of love and self-acceptance, *self-compassion* had to be the anchor of which I was doing the work. Self-compassion is not self-pity. Self-compassion is the ability to give yourself the grace, tenderness and love you would give anyone else. Self-compassion is recognizing the hardships that you have been through in life, and continuing to work on being the best version of yourself. Unlike self-pity, where you spend your time wallowing and blaming others for your misfortune, self-compassion is a healthy dose of accountability, self-forgiveness and the will to be different. When you are compassionate towards yourself, you can ground yourself in kindness even in moments where you feel like you are falling short. Healing is not linear, you will not feel healed and powerful all the time. Self-compassion is how you lovingly treat yourself in those moments of feeling like you have failed or reverted back to who you were. Self-compassion is your reminder that you too are human, you are not exempt from the human experience which entails making mistakes. Contrary to how you used to punish yourself when you did something outside of what you expected yourself to do, self-compassion is going to be your biggest teacher in lovingly redirecting the course.

Finally, we are going to make "no" your favorite word. You cannot be in the fullest pursuit of your authenticity and not learn how to set healthy boundaries with yourself and with those that you love. When you start your journey back to yourself, you are going to pay attention to how you engage with yourself and with your community. The first thing I want you to understand is that boundaries are not walls. When we set boundaries, we simply set rules for how we are going to be in a relationship with others, and how we are going to be in a relationship with ourselves. Boundaries are also flexible; they shift as we grow and evolve, whereas walls keep everyone and everything out. Although they give an illusion of emotional safety, walls keep everything out. They keep love, joy and community out while leaving us in a constant state of fear, discomfort and disconnection. Here are three things I really want you to know about setting boundaries:

1. We set boundaries with those we want to keep in our lives. Boundaries should never be a form of punishment for behavior that upsets you. They should instead be the guide

by which you foster healthy relationships that align with
who you are.

2. Boundaries require you to be compassionate and assertive.
   The underlying message about setting boundaries is that
   you are changing the rules of engagement and it will take
   time for people to change their behaviors. Instead of being
   upset and cutting them off, I ask you for compassion. You
   have been who you are for a really long time. These people
   have been in your life, engaging with you in a particular way
   for a long time too. So it will take time for them to learn and
   respect your boundaries. This is why you need to pair that
   compassion with being assertive. Just because they are
   struggling with respecting your boundaries doesn't mean
   you need to change them. It just means you might need to
   be okay with repeating yourself, and modeling what those
   boundaries are.

3. Be thoughtful about HOW you communicate with them. I
   tell my clients to set the stage for communicating their
   boundaries. Make sure that you are not communicating
   with them in times of conflict but rather during a time
   when no one's defenses are up. Yelling at people that they're
   not respecting boundaries you have not established is not
   going to make them respect your boundaries; rather, it will
   cause even further rifts in those relationships.

I often find myself thinking about my mother on this journey as a
coach, I think about what I would help her do if I was her coach. As a
trauma-informed coach, I would start by helping her unpack how that
trauma affected who she was as a wife and as a mother. Yes, my mother
self-sacrificed and self-abandoned, but she wasn't born like that. She
grew up in extreme poverty with a very strict mother. My stepfather was
not only an act of rebellion, but he was also her safe place. She was also
raised to believe that marriage was the ultimate achievement, and she
should do everything she possibly could to stay married, and boy did
she! I would help her rewrite the script that ultimately had her hustling
for love and connection - things that she didn't have growing up and

things that she believed needed to come from outside of her. I want you to know that your journey back to yourself is going to be full of overgrown weeds that you will need to uproot. Weeds that have latched on to your personhood forming the beliefs that you have about yourself. Those weeds are your trauma, your childhood wounds, the things you have buried and now must uproot in order to become who you have always known you are.

It's your turn, babe. Grab that pen and let's get to digging.

~

1. Who are you? I want you to define yourself outside of the relationships you're in or your job. When all that is stripped off of you, who are you?

_____
_____
_____
_____
_____
_____
_____
_____
_____
_____
_____
_____
_____
_____
_____
_____
_____
_____
_____
_____
_____
_____
_____
_____
_____
_____
_____
_____

2. Who do you want to be? The person you dream of becoming, who are they, how do they live? Where do they live? What do they do for fun?

_____

_____

_____

_____

_____

_____

_____

_____

_____

_____

_____

_____

_____

_____

_____

_____

_____

_____

_____

_____

_____

_____

_____

_____

_____

_____

_____

_____

3. What obstacles are standing between the person you are and the person you want to become?

4. In what areas of your life do you need to show yourself some compassion and why?

_____

_____

_____

_____

_____

_____

_____

_____

_____

_____

_____

_____

_____

_____

_____

_____

_____

_____

_____

_____

_____

_____

_____

_____

_____

_____

_____

_____

_____

_____

_____

5. What boundaries do you need to set in your life and with whom? How will these boundaries make those relationships healthy?

_____

_____

_____

_____

_____

_____

_____

_____

_____

_____

_____

_____

_____

_____

_____

_____

_____

_____

_____

_____

_____

_____

_____

_____

_____

_____

_____

_____

_____

_____

Babe, you have been everything to everyone for far too long. You have been the fixer, the one everyone dumps their baggage on and the baggage carrier for way too long. You have been the doormat, the scapegoat, the one who bears the brunt of life's challenges for others for way too long. You have been their emotional punching bag for way too long. You have also been lost, stuck and living on automatic for way too long. This uncomfortable feeling in your chest when you go to bed is trying to tell you that there is more to YOU than this. Your soul is begging you to return to you! It is time to stop being their martyr and become your own. It is time for you to start living your life, not surviving in it, not simply existing in it...but LIVING in it. This is your permission slip...

LIVE, SELFISHLY

CONCLUSION

"To be yourself in a world that is constantly trying to make you something else is the greatest accomplishment."

— RALPH WALDO EMERSON, AMERICAN ESSAYIST

A client once lamented to me that it is so difficult to do this self development work. She was in her third week of coaching with me and we were focusing on her negative self talk that was brought on by her self doubt. As a trauma-informed coach, I often make my clients dig deep into their childhoods and past experiences in order to understand the root cause of their struggles. I believe that without this as an integral part of the work, we are simply bandaging instead of truly healing and growing. What my client discovered was that she was repeating things to herself that her father used to say to *her* when she was a young girl. Her negative self talk was not hers, but his words. This is when she looked at me and said "this work is hard, coach." She was in tears at this point, facing the excruciating truth that she was never validated, or loved in the ways she needed to be loved as a child. What I reminded her at that point is the fact that *if this work was easy, everyone would be doing it.*

I want to extend the same reminder to you. We live in a world that greatly benefits from our conformity. Education and religious institutions would not function as they do if they taugth us to show up in this world as the most authentic versions of ourselves. They would crumble to their foundation if they had taught us the power of radical self love and self acceptance. Cultural norms and traditions are perpetuated through generations of forced uniformity and sameness. This society has a term for those of us who dare to swim against the tide - black sheep. It takes an incredible amount of work and intention to go against what you have been taught and choose to live the life of your own design. This work is hard because it has consequences. Choosing the path that leads to true personal determination and self actualization can be a lonely journey. You stand a chance of losing friends, family members and relationships you held dear to your heart will shift. That is hard. When you peel the masks off and let yourself be seen, you are at the risk of having the ones you love not like what they are looking at. That is hard.

But, here is the exciting part, you get to CHOOSE your hard. Yes, doing the work is hard, but so is staying the same. Having unrealised dreams is hard, staying in your comfort zone is hard, constantly hiding parts of yourself in order to fit in *IS* hard. You get to choose your hard. My hope for you is that you choose the hard that leads to freedom and fulfillment. I hope you choose the hard that is grounded in radical self love and self acceptance. I hope you choose the hard that gives birth to every single one of your wildest and audacious dreams. As you worked through this book, I hope you have felt the deep call to LIVE. I hope you gained clarity on who it is that you are, and who it is that you want to become. And I hope that you start your transformational journey and become who you know you are meant to be.

LIVE!

Thank You

If you have enjoyed or found value in this book, please take a moment to leave an honest/brief review on Amazon **amzn.to/3QY404W** or **Goodreads.** Your reviews help prospective readers decide if this is right for them & it is the greatest kindness you can offer the author.

Thank you in advance.

Acknowledgments

Indy, you listened to me dream of this book for years, you encouraged me to be attentive, to be clear and to be slow. You loved me through the ups and down of this creation and held me up through self doubt - how can I not thank you!

My grandparents who spent countless nights under a dying candle and listened to me dream about a different life, thank you for allowing me to dream and manifest a different reality from yours.

My mother, you were the brightest of lights and even in your death, you still shine so bright. Thank you for teaching me what strength and grace feel like.

My aunt, Nomandla, I take nothing for granted, thank you for all you have been in life.

My chosen sister, Nina, bet you didn't think I'd thank you here! You are more than a best friend, thank you for how you celebrate me and thank you for how you hold me down.

To you, my readers, thank you for purchasing, reading and reviewing this work. I write for you. I create for you.

About the Author

Khanyisa Mnyaka is a Self Love Coach, TEDx Speaker, and Humanitarian. Her work is centered on empowering individuals to live as their most confident, empowered and authentic selves.

https://khanyisamnyaka.com/

instagram.com/lifecoachkhanyi

tiktok.com/@lifecoachkhanyi

ALSO BY KHANYISA MNYAKA

Traveling While Black and Lesbian

Traveling While Black And Lesbian is a raw and honest story about a queer, black woman's journey around the world and her struggle to navigate it as her authentic self. Khanyisa begins this "tell all" by bringing us into her childhood. She transports us to her life as a little girl growing up poor in rural South Africa, being the first generation of black children to live in post-apartheid South Africa, her conflict with her sexual identity and religion, her battle with depression and loss.

As a traveler that is queer, black and female – Khanyisa has experienced the complexities of negotiating ones different identities in different parts of the world. We watch her come out of the closet in South Korea, find deep connections with her Muslim friends in Malaysia, walk in spiritual presence at the Mayan ruins in Guatemala, and so much more. Khanyisa also brings into her intimate relationships – we bear witness to her falling in love, getting her heartbroken and picking up the pieces. This is a true testimony of triumph, human connection, and the return to oneself.

In this memoir, we learn the true power that lies within each of us when we finally begin to embrace our true and authentic selves.

RED THREAD PUBLISHING
ABOUT THE PUBLISHER

Red Thread Publishing is an all-female publishing company on a mission to support 10,000 folx to become successful published authorpreneurs & thought leaders.

To work with us or connect regarding any of our growing library of books email us at **info@redthreadbooks.com.**

To learn more about us visit our website **www.redthreadbooks.com.**

Follow us & join the community.

facebook.com/redthreadpublishing

instagram.com/redthreadbooks

Made in United States
North Haven, CT
19 June 2024

53847250R00102